Pork

BLOOMSBURY KITCHEN LIBRARY

Pork

Bloomsbury Books
London

This edition published 1994 by Bloomsbury Books,
an imprint of The Godfrey Cave Group,
42 Bloomsbury Street, London, WC1B 3QJ.

ISBN 1 85471 547 X

Printed and bound in Great Britain.

Contents

Tea Pork Chops with Two Purées

Serves 4

Working time: about 40 minutes

Total time: about 3 hours (includes marinating)

Calories 340
Protein 36g
Cholesterol 70mg
Total fat 11g
Saturated fat 5g
Sodium 310mg

8	boneless middle-loin chops (about 125 g/4 oz each), trimmed of fat	**8**	
8	shallots, finely chopped	**8**	
12.5 cl	red wine	**4 fl oz**	
45 cl	unsalted veal stock	**¾ pint**	
300 g	sweet potatoes	**10 oz**	
350 g	broccoli florets	**10 oz**	
90 g	fromage frais	**3 oz**	
½ tsp	salt	**½ tsp**	

freshly ground black pepper

Cardamom Marinade

5 tbsp	unsalted veal stock or water	**5 tbsp**
2½ tsp	strong Indian tea leaves	**2½ tsp**
32	cardamom pods	**32**
½	lemon, grated rind only	**½**
½ tsp	salt	**½ tsp**
	freshly ground black pepper	

For the marinade, bring the stock to the boil. Remove from the heat, add tea, cover and infuse for 3 mins. Strain into a bowl, add remaining ingredients. Cover; cool for 30 mins. Remove cardamom pods and press open; scrape out the seeds and crush them; return all to the liquid. Place the pork in a dish, pour on marinade, cover and leave in a cool place for 2 hrs, turning once.

After 1½ hrs, sauté shallots until transparent, add wine and simmer until pan is almost dry. Add stock, boil and simmer to reduce by ½ – 20 mins.

Remove chops from the marinade and pat dry. Strain the marinade; reserve some of the pods. Add ½ of the marinade to the reduced sauce,

boil, then simmer until a light syrupy consistency. Strain through a fine sieve and keep warm.

In a dry frying pan, sear the meat over high heat for 2 mins on each side. Reduce the heat and cook for 10 mins, turning once. Remove the meat from the pan and leave in a low oven.

Meanwhile, steam the sweet potatoes and broccoli in separate pans until tender. Purée separately. Blend ½ of the *fromage frais* into each purée and season.

Serve two chops per person with sauce poured over and cardamom pod garnish. Serve the two purées separately.

Chops with Redcurrant Sauce

Serves 4

Working
(and total)
time: about
20 minutes

Calories
245

Protein
29g

Cholesterol
60mg

Total fat
9g

Saturated fat
4g

Sodium
270mg

4	pork chops (125 to 150 g/4½ to 5 oz each), trimmed of fat	4
500 g	redcurrants, washed	1 lb
	freshly ground black pepper	
½ tbsp	safflower oil	½ tbsp
2½ tbsp	redcurrant or raspberry vinegar	2½ tbsp
2 tbsp	redcurrant jelly	2 tbsp
½ tsp	salt	½ tsp

Reserve a few whole redcurrants for a garnish, and pass the remainder through a sieve. Discard the contents of the sieve and reserve the sieved purée.

Season the meat on both sides with some pepper, rubbing it in with your fingers. Heat the oil in a heavy frying pan over high heat and, when it is smoking, add the chops. Brown them quickly on both sides and reduce the heat to very low. Continue cooking, turning occasionally, until the meat is firm but still springy when you press it with your finger – about 7 minutes. Remove the chops from the pan and keep them warm.

Deglaze the pan with the vinegar, and cook over high heat until the vinegar has almost evaporated. Add the redcurrant purée and jelly to the pan, and reduce for about 1 minute; add the salt. Serve the chops with the sauce and the reserved whole redcurrants spooned round them.

Stuffed Pork Chops with Calvados

Serves 4

Working time: about 30 minutes

Total time: about 45 minutes

Calories 375

Protein 29g

Cholesterol 70mg

Total fat 14g

Saturated fat 4g

Sodium 270mg

4	boneless pork chops (about 125 g/ 4 oz each), trimmed of fat	**4**
3	dessert apples	**3**
1 tbsp	finely chopped fresh thyme, or 1 tsp dried thyme	**1 tbsp**
	freshly ground black pepper	
3 tbsp	fresh lemon juice	**3 tbsp**
1½ tbsp	safflower oil	**1½ tbsp**
12.5 cl	calvados	**4 fl oz**
1½ tbsp	single cream	**1½ tbsp**
½ tsp	salt	**½ tsp**

Make a small incision in the side of each chop and carefully cut a pocket. Peel, core and slice one apple finely, sprinkle half of the thyme over the slices and press them into the cavities in the chops. Season the chops with some pepper, rubbing it in with your fingers. Peel, core and slice the remaining apples, not so finely, and sprinkle with the lemon juice to prevent them from discolouring.

Heat half of the oil in a heavy or non-stick frying pan over high heat. When it hot but not smoking, add the chops and brown for 1 minute on each side. Remove the pan from the heat and allow the chops to sizzle for another 3 minutes, turning once. Remove the chops from the pan and keep them warm.

Heat the remaining oil in the frying pan, and add the apples and the remaining thyme. Cook gently over medium heat until the apples are almost soft. Remove from the heat. Add the calvados and, when the sizzling has stopped, return to the heat and cook for 1 minute. Add the cream and allow to bubble up once. Replace the chops in the pan, pouring in any juices that have collected; add the salt, warm through and serve.

Suggested accompaniment: parslied carrots.

Editor's Note: The softness of the fried apples should contrast pleasantly with the crunch of those inside the chops.

Stir-Fried Pork and Squid

Serves 4

Working time: about 25 minutes

Total time: about 1 hour (includes marinating)

Calories 200

Protein 23g

Cholesterol 205mg

Total fat 10g

Saturated fat 2g

Sodium 320mg

250 g	pork fillet, trimmed of fat and cut into thin strips	8 oz
250 g	squid, cut into thin strips	8 oz
1 tbsp	low-sodium soy sauce or shoyu	1 tbsp
1 tbsp	dry sherry	1 tbsp
16	spring onions	16
1 tsp	cornflour	1 tsp
4 tbsp	unsalted vegetable stock or water	4 tbsp
1 tbsp	arachide or safflower oil	1 tbsp
1 tsp	sesame oil	1 tsp
2 tsp	finely chopped fresh ginger root	2 tsp

Put the strips of pork and squid in a non-reactive dish with the soy sauce and sherry, and leave to marinate for 45 minutes. Cut the spring onions in half and slice some green tops into julienne for a garnish. Remove the pork and squid from the marinade and set them aside. Mix the cornflour and the stock or water into the marinade.

Heat the oils together in a wok or heavy frying pan until they are hot but not smoking, add the ginger and stir-fry for 1 minute. Add the pork and squid and stir-fry for 4 minutes; then add the spring onions and cook for another 2 minutes. Pour in the marinade mixture, cook for a final minute, and serve at once, garnished with the spring onion julienne.

Stir-Fried Pork with Mange-Tout

250 g	pork fillet, trimmed of fat and cut into 5 mm (¼ inch) thickstrips	**8 oz**
5	dried shiitake mushrooms, soaked in water for 20 to 30 minutes	**5**
12	baby sweetcorn	**12**
3	spring onions	**3**
2 tsp	safflower oil	**2 tsp**
1	garlic clove, crushed	**1**
1 cm	fresh ginger root, cut into fine julienne	**½ inch**
200 g	bamboo shoots, thinly sliced lengthwise	**7 oz**

200 g	mange-tout	**7 oz**
1 tsp	low-sodium soy sauce or shoyu	**1 tsp**
1 tsp	dry or medium-dry sherry	**1 tsp**
2 tbsp	unsalted veal stock or water	**2 tbsp**
1 tsp	cornflour or potato flour, mixed with 4 tsp cold water	**1 tsp**
1	small carrot, sliced into fine julienne	**1**
	Sherry Marinade	
1 tsp	low-sodium soy sauce or shoyu	**1 tsp**
1 tsp	dry or medium-dry sherry	**1 tsp**
1 tsp	cornflour or potato flour white pepper	**1 tsp**

Combine marinade ingredients in a dish. Add pork, coat evenly, marinate for 20 mins.

Strain the mushroom-soaking liquid and reserve; squeeze mushrooms dry and slice thinly. Blanch the sweetcorn for 5 mins in salted boiling water with a squeeze of lemon, refresh in cold water and drain. Shred the spring onions along the grain and put in iced water; when curled, drain.

Heat 1 tsp oil in a wok and stir-fry the pork over medium-high until light brown. Remove pork and drain in a sieve over a bowl.

Heat remaining oil until smoking and add the garlic. Discard garlic when brown, add ginger, bamboo and mushrooms. Stir-fry for 3 mins, add mange-tout and stir-fry for a further 3 mins.

Reduce heat, add soy sauce, sherry, stock, mushroom liquid and any juices from the pork. Increase heat, cook for 2 to 3 mins; add cornflour mixture, stir until it thickens and turns translucent. Add pork and sweetcorn to the wok and heat for 1 min, remove wok from heat, stir in the carrot.

Serve, with spring onion curls for garnish.

Pork and Ginger Stir-Fry Salad

Serves 4

Working time: about 35 minutes

Total time: about 50 minutes

Calories
235

Protein
23g

Cholesterol
70mg

Total fat
14g

Saturated fat
4g

Sodium
205mg

500 g	pork fillet, trimmed of fat and cut into thin strips	**1 lb**
1 tbsp	sesame oil	**1 tbsp**
1	garlic clove, crushed	**1**
2.5 cm	piece fresh ginger root, finely chopped	**1 inch**
1 tsp	chili sauce	**1 tsp**
2 tbsp	low-sodium soy sauce or shoyu	**2 tbsp**
3	shallots, thinly sliced	**3**
$\frac{1}{8}$ tsp	five-spice powder	**$\frac{1}{8}$ tsp**
1 tbsp	safflower oil	**1 tbsp**
1	sweet red pepper, seeded, deribbed and cut into thin strips	**1**

	Lettuce and Bean Sprout Salad	
$\frac{1}{2}$	small red oakleaf lettuce, washed and dried	**$\frac{1}{2}$**
6	curly endive leaves, washed and dried	**6**
1	bunch watercress, washed, stems trimmed	**1**
4	Chinese cabbage leaves, washed dried and shredded	**4**
4	spring onions, sliced diagonally	**4**
125 g	bean sprouts	**4 oz**

In a large, non-reactive bowl, mix the sesame oil with the garlic, ginger, chili sauce, soy sauce, shallots and five-spice powder. Add the pork strips and mix well. Cover and marinate for at least 15 minutes.

Meanwhile, prepare the salad. Arrange the oakleaf lettuce, curly endive leaves and watercress sprigs in a border round a serving dish. Mix the shredded chinese cabbage with the spring onions and bean sprouts, and place the mixture in the centre of the dish.

Heat the safflower oil in a large heavy frying pan. Add the pork and its marinade, and cook over fairly high heat for about 4 minutes, stirring all the time. Add the red pepper strips and cook for a further 1 to 2 minutes, again stirring all the time. Pile the hot pork mixture over the prepared salad and serve at once.

Stir-Fried Liver in Orange and Brandy Sauce

Serves 4

Working (and total) time: about 15 minutes

Calories
340

Protein
29g

Cholesterol
235mg

Total fat
18g

Saturated fat
5g

Sodium
290mg

350 g	pig's liver, thinly sliced	**12 oz**
2 tbsp	safflower oil	**2 tbsp**
2	onions, sliced	**2**
1	sweet green pepper, seeded, deribbed and sliced	**1**
1	garlic clove, chopped	**1**
1 tbsp	plain flour	**1 tbsp**
2 tbsp	tomato paste	**2 tbsp**
3	oranges, two peeled, halved and sliced, juice only of the third	**3**
12.5 cl	unsalted vegetable stock	**4 fl oz**
½ tsp	salt	**½ tsp**
	freshly ground black pepper	
2 tbsp	brandy	**2 tbsp**
3 tbsp	single cream (optional)	**3 tbsp**

Heat the oil in a wok or large heavy frying pan over high heat and cook the liver until it has coloured – 3 to 4 minutes. Remove the liver from the pan and set it aside while you make the sauce.

Add the sliced onions, green pepper and garlic to the pan and cook over low heat for 5 to 10 minutes to soften them. Stir in the flour and tomato paste, then gradually add the orange juice and vegetable stock. Season with the salt and some freshly ground pepper and bring to the boil, stirring continuously.

Reserve a few orange slices for a garnish; add the remaining slices of orange to the pan with the cooked liver and the brandy, and heat through for another minute. Remove the pan from the heat and stir in the cream, if you are using it. Serve the liver garnished with the reserved orange slices.

Suggested accompaniment: plain boiled rice.

Medallions of Pork with Two Green Purées

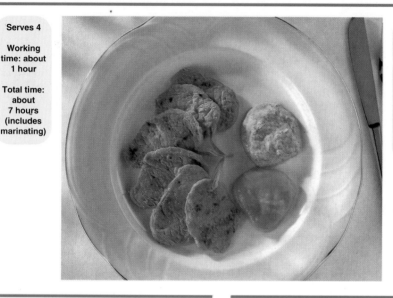

Serves 4

Working time: about 1 hour

Total time: about 7 hours (includes marinating)

Calories 290
Protein 25g
Cholesterol 70mg
Total fat 18g
Saturated fat 4g
Sodium 185mg

500 g	pork fillet, trimmed of fat	1 lb
2	large green sweet peppers, seeded and deribbed	2
2 tsp	green peppercorns, rinsed and drained if bottled	2 tsp
4 cm	piece fresh ginger root	1½ inch
2 tbsp	virgin olive oil	2 tbsp
1 tbsp	wine vinegar	1 tbsp
¼ tsp	salt	¼ tsp
500 g	fresh sharp gooseberries	1 lb
2	fresh mint sprigs	2
1 tbsp	fructose	1 tbsp
60 g	fresh sorrel	2 oz
150 g	fromage frais	5 oz

Slice the fillet into 20 thin rounds, then beat them out until they are about half as large again.

Mix the green peppers, peppercorns, two thirds of the ginger, half the oil, the vinegar and salt in a processer. Coat meat with this marinade and leave in a dish for about 6 hours at room temperature (or 12 hours in the refrigerator).

To prepare the two purées, first wash and cook the gooseberries in a little water with the mint and fructose, until they are soft. Drain the cooked gooseberries and pass them through a sieve or purée them in a food processor or blender. If using a food processor or blender, sieve the purée after processing.

Wash the sorrel and strip the leaves from the stems. Cook the leaves with a little additional water until they are broken down and almost puréed. Beat the sorrel into the fromage frais and, using a garlic press, squeeze the juice from the remaining piece of fresh ginger into the mixture (or grate the ginger finely, sieve it, and add to the mixture). Keep the two purées warm in bowls set in pans of simmering water.

Wipe the marinade ingredients off the pieces of meat. Heat half of the remaining oil in a frying pan and cook half of the meat gently for up to 1 minute on each side; browning is not essential. Remove, and keep warm while cooking the second batch in the oil. Serve the medallions immediately, accompanied by the purées.

Noisettes in a Sherry Vinegar Sauce

Serves 4

Working (and total) time: about 20 minutes

Calories
270

Protein
24g

Cholesterol
70mg

Total fat
14g

Saturated fat
5g

Sodium
320mg

500 g	pork fillet, trimmed of fat and cut into 16 slices	**1 lb**
	freshly ground black pepper	
1 tbsp	virgin olive oil	**1 tbsp**
10	garlic cloves, peeled	**10**
3 tbsp	sherry or red wine vinegar	**3 tbsp**
1 tbsp	dry sherry	**1 tbsp**

2 tbsp	unsalted chicken or veal stock	**2 tbsp**
750 g	ripe tomatoes, skinned, seeded and chopped, or 400 g (14 oz) canned whole tomatoes, drained	**1½ lb**
15 g	unsalted butter (optional)	**½ oz**
¼ tsp	salt	**¼ tsp**
30 g	finely chopped parsley or chives	**1 oz**

Season the pork generously with pepper, pressing it in with your fingers. Heat the oil in a heavy frying pan over high heat and, when it is smoking, add the pork. Brown the pork quickly on both sides and reduce the heat to very low. Add the garlic. Continue cooking until the pork is firm but still springy when you press it with a finger – 5 to 8 minutes, depending on thickness. Remove the pork from the pan and keep it warm.

Increase the heat and deglaze the pan with the vinegar. When it has all but disappeared, add the sherry and reduce for about 1 minute.

Add the stock and tomatoes, and cook over high heat until reduced by half. Remove from the heat and pass the mixture through a sieve. Lower the heat, return the sauce and the meat to the pan and reheat briefly; if you wish, add the butter, off the heat, to thicken the sauce.

Season the pork with the salt, arrange it on four plates and spoon the sauce round it. Garnish with the chopped parsley or chives before serving.

Suggested accompaniment: French beans.

Patties with Aubergine Purée

Serves 4

Working
(and total)
time: about
30 minutes

Calories
220
Protein
23g
Cholesterol
70mg
Total fat
12g
Saturated fat
4g
Sodium
120mg

450 g	trimmed leg or neck end of pork, minced	15 oz	1¼ tsp	cumin seeds	1¼ tsp
20 g	spring onion, white part only, finely chopped	¾ oz	1	shallot, finely chopped	1
2 tsp	ground coriander	2 tsp	45 g	fromage frais	1½ oz
500 g	aubergines	1 lb		freshly ground black pepper	
			1 tbsp	safflower oil	1 tbsp
				fresh coriander sprigs, for garnish	

Mix the minced pork with the finely chopped spring onions and ground coriander, and form it into eight patties measuring about 6 cm (2½ inches) in diameter.

Cut the aubergines in half lengthwise and place them in a vegetable steamer. Lay a sheet of greaseproof paper over the top, and steam until they are tender – about 10 minutes.

Heat the cumin seeds in a non-stick frying pan over medium heat, stirring frequently, for about 3 minutes. Add the finely chopped shallot and cook it until it has softened. Scoop the flesh from the aubergine halves and purée it in

a food processor or a blender, together with the contents of the frying pan. Return the mixture to the pan, and stir in the *fromage frais* and some freshly ground black pepper.

Heat the oil in another non-stick frying pan, over high heat, and brown the pork patties for 2 minutes on each side, then reduce the heat and cook for a further 3 minutes. Meanwhile, gently warm the purée over low heat, stirring constantly.

Spoon the purée on to four warmed plates. Place two pork patties on each plate and garnish with the sprigs of coriander.

Porkburgers

Serves 4

Working
(and total)
time: about
35 minutes

Calories
340

Protein
32g

Cholesterol
85mg

Total fat
12g

Saturated fat
4g

Sodium
550mg

250 g	pork fillet, trimmed of fat and minced	**8 oz**
250 g	topside of veal, trimmed of fat and minced	**8 oz**
1	onion, very finely chopped	**1**
¼ tsp	salt	**¼ tsp**
½ tsp	dry mustard	**½ tsp**
¼ tsp	chili powder	**¼ tsp**
1 tbsp	safflower oil	**1 tbsp**
4	wholemeal baps, split in half	**4**

4	crisp lettuce leaves, washed and dried	**4**
4	slices beef tomato	**4**
4	mild or hot pickled chili peppers	**4**
	Chili Topping	
4 tbsp	chili relish	**4 tbsp**
1	carrot, grated	**1**
2	shallots, finely chopped	**2**
2.5 cm	piece cucumber, finely chopped	**1 inch**

In a bowl, mix the pork with the veal, onion, salt, dry mustard and chili powder. Form the mixture into four burger shapes about 1 cm (½ inch) thick.

Heat the oil in a large heavy frying pan over medium heat. Add the pork burgers and cook them for 5 to 6 minutes on each side.

Meanwhile, make the topping. In a bowl, mix the chili relish with the carrot, shallots and cucumber. Warm the baps under a medium-hot grill.

Arrange a lettuce leaf on the base portion of each bap, then add a porkburger to each, and top with a slice of tomato and a spoonful of chili topping. Cover the bap lids and secure them in position with cocktail sticks. Garnish the burgers with the pickled chili peppers, and serve at once.

Pepper Pork with Mozzarella

Serves 4

Working time: about 25 minutes

Total time: about 40 minutes

Calories 240

Protein 25g

Cholesterol 90mg

Total fat 14g

Saturated fat 5g

Sodium 225mg

500 g	pork fillet, trimmed of fat	1 lb		2	shallots, finely chopped	2
1 tsp	green peppercorns	1 tsp			Tabasco sauce	
1 tsp	black peppercorns	1 tsp			Worcester sauce	
1 tbsp	safflower oil	1 tbsp		15 cl	unsalted chicken stock	¼ pint
1	garlic clove, halved	1		2 tbsp	dry sherry	2 tbsp
60 g	low-fat mozzarella, grated	2 oz		4	flat-leaf parsley sprigs	4

Lay the pork fillet on a board and, with a sharp knife, cut it at a slightly diagonal angle into 12 slices, each about 2 cm (¾ inch) wide. Crush the green and black peppercorns using a pestle and mortar. Sprinkle the pepper over one side of the pork slices and press it into the meat. Cover, and set aside for 15 minutes.

Heat the oil in a large frying pan over medium heat. Add the garlic and the pork slices, peppered side down, and cook over medium heat for 3 to 4 minutes on each side, until well browned. Preheat the grill. Remove the pork from the pan and arrange the slices, peppered side up, in two slightly overlapping rows in a shallow proof serving dish. Sprinkle the pork with the

mozzarella and cook under the grill until the cheese has melted and is beginning to brown.

Meanwhile, discard the garlic from the frying pan. Add the shallots to the pan and stir well, scraping up any sediment from the bottom of the pan. Stir in a few drops each of Tabasco sauce and Worcester sauce, and add the stock and sherry. Simmer the sauce for about 3 minutes, until slightly reduced. Spoon the sauce round the pork steaks and serve at once, garnished with the parsley sprigs

Suggested accompaniments: tiny new potatoes; watercress, curly endive and green pepper salad.

Escalopes with Tomato and Mozzarella

Serves 4

Working time: about 20 minutes

Total time: about 40 minutes

Calories 295
Protein 25g
Cholesterol 70mg
Total fat 18g
Saturated fat 6g
Sodium 290mg

4	pork escalopes (about 100 g/3½ oz each), trimmed of fat	4
2 tbsp	virgin olive oil	2 tbsp
1	small onion, finely chopped	1
1	small carrot, finely chopped	1
½	stick celery, finely chopped	½
750 g	ripe tomatoes, skinned and seeded, or 400 g (14 oz) canned tomatoes, drained	1½ lb
1 tbsp	tomato paste	1 tbsp
2	bay leaves	2
	freshly ground black pepper	
45 g	fresh basil, chopped	1½ oz
75 g	low-fat mozzarella, thinly sliced	2½ oz

Heat 1 tablespoon of the oil in heavy-bottomed or non-stick saucepan and gently cook the chopped onion, carrot and celery until softened – about 3 minutes. Add the tomatoes, tomato paste and the bay leaves to the pan and cook for about 20 minutes, or until the sauce is no longer runny, stirring frequently.

Preheat the grill to high. Season the escalopes with some freshly ground pepper, rubbing it in with your fingertips. In a heavy or non-stick frying pan, heat the remaining oil over high heat until it is smoking, and brown the escalopes on both sides for 1 minute. Remove the pan from the heat an allow the meat to sizzle for a couple of minutes, turning once.

Transfer the escalopes to a grill rack and spread over them equal portions of the tomato sauce, then sprinkle with the basil and top with the mozzarella. Heat under the hot grill for 1 minute or until the cheese has melted. Serve immediately.

Suggested accompaniment: plain boiled rice and green salad.

Pork with a Passion Fruit Sauce

Serves 4		Calories 260
Working time: about 15 minutes		**Protein 32g**
		Cholesterol 70mg
Total time: about 3 hours and 15 minutes (includes marinating)		**Total fat 11g**
		Saturated fat 4g
		Sodium 110mg

4	pork loin steaks (about 125 g/4 oz each), trimmed of fat	4	**17.5 cl**	dry white wine	**6 fl oz**
4	passion fruit	4		white pepper	
			1 tsp	sugar (optional)	**1 tsp**

Beat the steaks with a mallet to flatten them slightly, then place them in a single layer in a shallow non-reactive dish.

Squeeze the juice from the passion fruit; reserve the seeds. Pour the juice on to the pork and spread the seeds over the surface. Cover the dish and leave in a cool place for 3 hours, turning the pork frequently.

Preheat the grill to very high. Remove the pork from the marinade and brush off any seeds adhering to it; reserve the marinade. Place the steaks close to the source of heat and grill for about 4 minutes on each side, until lightly charred on the surface but still tender in the centre.

Meanwhile, in a small pan, boil the wine until it is reduced to about 4 tablespoons, then stir in the reserved marinade and heat through. Taste the sauce and add the sugar if desired; season with some white pepper. Serve the pork with the sauce spooned over.

Editor's Note: If preferred, the passion fruit juice may be strained and the seeds discarded.

Indian Chops

Serves 4

Working time: about 25 minutes

Total time: about 1 day (includes marinating)

Calories 290

Protein 40g

Cholesterol 70mg

Total fat 14g

Saturated fat 5g

Sodium 225mg

4	pork chops (about 175 g/6 oz each), trimmed of fat	4
1	fresh chili pepper, or dried chili pepper soaked in water for 30 minutes seeded and chopped,	1
2	garlic cloves	2

1	small piece turmeric	1
$\frac{1}{2}$ tsp	fenugreek seeds	$\frac{1}{2}$ tsp
$\frac{1}{2}$ tsp	coriander seeds	$\frac{1}{2}$ tsp
$\frac{1}{2}$ tsp	cumin seeds	$\frac{1}{2}$ tsp
$\frac{1}{2}$ tsp	salt	$\frac{1}{2}$ tsp
4 tbsp	plain low-fat yogurt	4 tbsp

Using a mortar and pestle, pound the chili pepper with the garlic, tumeric and other seasonings into a coarse paste. Mix the yogurt into the paste and blend well.

Coat the pork chops with the yogurt mixture, place them in a non-reactive dish, cover with plastic film and leave to marinate in the refrigerator for 24 hours.

Preheat the grill to very hot. Remove the chops from the marinade, wipe them with paper towels and brush off any dry ingredients that are sticking to them. Heat two metal skewers over high heat on the stove and print a criss-cross pattern on both sides of each chop by pressing the skewer gently on to the surface.

Cook the chops for 7 minutes on each side, or until cooked through. Leave the chops in a warm place to rest for 5 minutes before serving.

Suggested accompaniments: new potatoes tossed in toasted poppy seeds; cucumber in yogurt and mint dressing.

Editor's Note: Ground spices may be substituted for the tumeric stem and the fenugreek, coriander and cumin seeds, but grinding the ingredients in a mortar yields a better flavour. About $\frac{1}{2}$ teaspoon of mustard powder may be used instead of the chili peppers. If you barbecue the chops on a grid over charcoal, you do not need to sear them with a skewer.

Pork Chops with Kumquats

Serves 4

Working
time: about
20 minutes

Total time:
about
2 hours and
20 minutes
(includes
marinating)

Calories
320
Protein
33g
Cholesterol
80mg
Total fat
13g
Saturated fat
6g
Sodium
280mg

4	pork chops (125 to 150 g/4½ to 5 oz each), trimmed of fat	4
6 tbsp	dry white wine or vermouth	6 tbsp
6 tbsp	fresh orange juice	6 tbsp
2 tsp	clear honey	2 tsp

250 g	ripe kumquats	8 oz
½ tsp	salt	½ tsp
	freshly ground black pepper	
15 g	unsalted butter, chilled	½ oz

Combine the wine or vermouth with the orange juice and honey in a non-reactive dish. Add the pork and leave to marinate for at least 2 hours.

Remove the meat from the dish and reserve the marinade. Pat the meat dry with paper towels and set it aside. Preheat the grill.

Reserve four kumquats for garnish; purée the rest in a food processor with the reserved marinade, then pass it through a fine sieve. In a small pan over high heat, reduce the purée for about 1 minute or until thick and bright orange. Remove from the heat.

Season the pork with the salt and a little pepper and cook under the hot grill for 5 minutes on each side, or until cooked through. Reheat the sauce then, off the heat, whisk in the chilled butter to thicken it. Serve the chops with the sauce spooned round them, garnished with thin slices of the reserved kumquats.

Kebabs in Tea and Ginger Marinade

Serves 4

Working time: about 35 minutes

Total time: about 9 hours (includes marinating)

Calories 160
Protein 22g
Cholesterol 70mg
Total fat 8g
Saturated fat 3g
Sodium 80mg

500 g	pork fillet, trimmed of fat and cut into 24 cubes	1 lb
16	shallots, peeled, or spring onion bulbs	16
16	button mushrooms	16

Tea Marinade

1 tsp	Earl Grey tea leaves	1 tsp
1	garlic clove, crushed	1
2 tbsp	finely chopped fresh ginger root	2 tbsp
4 tbsp	dry sherry	4 tbsp
1 tbsp	light brown sugar	1 tbsp
2 tbsp	virgin olive oil	2 tbsp

To make the marinade, put the tea leaves in a jug and pour 12.5 cl (4 fl oz) of boiling water over them. Leave to steep for 4 minutes, then strain into a bowl. Add the remaining marinade ingredients to the bowl and stir to mix well.

Add the pork cubes to the bowl and turn to coat with the marinade. Cover the bowl and put it in the refrigerator for 8 hours, or overnight.

When ready to cook, preheat the grill. Drain the meat, reserving the marinade. Thread the pork cubes alternating with the shallots and mushrooms on to eight skewers. Brush all over

with the marinade and grill, about 12.5 cm (5 inches) from the source of heat, for 15 minutes, turning to cook evenly and basting frequently with the reserved marinade. Serve hot.

Suggested accompaniment: puréed swedes.

Editor's Note: If you use wooden skewers, soak them in water for about 10 minutes before threading them with the pork and vegetables to prevent them from burning under the grill.

Devilled Medallions

Serves 4

Working time: about 25 minutes

Total time: about 35 minutes

Calories 275
Protein 25g
Cholesterol 70mg
Total fat 8g
Saturated fat 3g
Sodium 320mg

500 g	boned pork loin, trimmed of fat and cut into eight medallions (about 1 cm/½ inch thick)	**1 lb**
2 tbsp	Dijon mustard	**2 tbsp**
3 tbsp	dry white wine	**3 tbsp**
½ tsp	hot paprika	**½ tsp**
	freshly ground black pepper	

175 g	fine dry brown breadcrumbs	**6 oz**
	Peach Chutney	
2	ripe peaches (about 250 g/8 oz)	**2**
1 tbsp	capers, chopped	**1 tbsp**
1–2	spring onions, finely chopped	**1–2**
1 tbsp	fresh lemon juice	**1 tbsp**

First make the chutney. Peel and stone both peaches, then purée one peach in a blender or food procesor and pour into a bowl. Chop the other peach roughly and stir it into the purée with the capers, spring onions and lemon juice. Set aside.

Combine the mustard, wine, paprika and some black pepper in a shallow dish. Stir well until smooth. Spread out the breadcrumbs on a plate or a sheet of greaseproof paper. Dip the medallions, one at a time, in the mustard mixture and gently shake off excess, then coat both sides and round the edges with the crumbs, pressing them down with the blade of a table knife. Leave the coated medallions to dry briefly while you preheat the grill.

Grill the medallions under moderately high heat, about 12.5 cm (5 inches) from the heat source, for 5 minutes on each side, or until they are lightly browned and the pork is cooked through.

Arrange the medallions on a warm platter or individual plates. Serve with the chutney.

Pork Char-Shiu

Serves 4

Working time: about 30 minutes

Total time: about 3 hours and 30 minutes (includes marinating)

Calories 230

Protein 27g

Cholesterol 90mg

Total fat 9g

Saturated fat 4g

Sodium 100mg

2	pork fillets (about 300 g/10 oz each), thin ends cut off, trimmed of fat	2
2 tbsp	low-sodium soy sauce or shoyu	2 tbsp
3–4	spring onions, finely chopped	3–4
2.5 cm	piece fresh ginger root, finely chopped	1 inch
2	garlic cloves, finely chopped	2
½ tsp	Sichuan pepper	½ tsp
2	star anise	2
1 tbsp	dry sherry	1 tbsp
1 tbsp	honey	1 tbsp
1½ tsp	red wine vinegar	1½ tsp
½ tsp	cornflour or potato flour, mixed with 2 tbsp water	½ tsp
	mixed salad leaves, washed and dried	

Rub the pork with 1 tablespoon of the soy sauce and leave for 20 minutes in a cool place. In a mortar, pound the spring onions, ginger and garlic to a rough paste with the Sichuan pepper and star anise. Mix in the sherry, the remaining soy sauce, half of the honey and 1 teaspoon of the vinegar; coat the pork with the paste and leave it to marinate for 2 to 6 hours in the refrigerator, turning it once or twice.

Remove the pork from the refrigerator, pat it dry with paper towels and discard any dry ingredients that are sticking to it. Strain the marinade and reserve. Prepare a glazing syrup by mixing 1 teaspoon of hot water with the remaining honey and vinegar.

Preheat the grill to very hot, place the meat close to the source of heat and brown it on both sides for 3 to 4 minutes. Move the meat to about 10 cm (4 inches) from the heat source and continue to cook for a further 10 minutes, turning a few times and basting constantly with the glazing syrup. Test for doneness with a skewer – the juice that runs out should be almost clear. Cover the cooked fillet loosely with aluminium foil, and leave to rest for 5 minutes.

Heat the reserved marinade to a simmer, add the cornflour and bring back to a simmer. To serve, cut the fillet across the grain into thin slices and place on a bed of salad leaves. Serve the marinade seperately as a dipping sauce.

Pork Kofta

Serves 4

Working time: about 35 minutes

Total time: about 2 hours and 30 minutes (includes marinating)

Calories 375

Protein 30g

Cholesterol 80mg

Total fat 20g

Saturated fat 5g

Sodium 510mg

500 g	minced pork fillet	**1 lb**
1	lemon, grated rind only	**1**
2	garlic cloves, crushed	**2**
1 tbsp	coriander seeds, toasted and coarsely ground	**1 tbsp**
½ tsp	salt	**½ tsp**
	freshly ground black pepper	
3 tbsp	dry white wine	**3 tbsp**
1½ tbsp	fresh lemon juice	**1½ tbsp**
1½ tbsp	virgin olive oil	**1½ tbsp**
4	carrots, grated	**4**
30 g	fresh coriander leaves, chopped	**1 oz**
4	pitta breads	**4**

Combine the pork with the lemon rind, garlic, coriander seeds, salt and some pepper. Divide into four and roll into sausage shapes about 15 by 2.5 cm (6 by 1 inch). Gently place the kofta in a shallow dish and pour on the wine, 1 tablespoon of the lemon juice and the oil. Leave to marinate for at least 2 hours, turning the kofta and coating with the marinade at frequent intervals.

Preheat the grill to high. Mix the carrots with the coriander leaves and the remaining lemon juice.

Remove the kofta from the marinade and grill them until the pork feels firm and is well browned on all sides – about 7 minutes. Meanwhile, warm the pitta bread through in a 170°C (325°F or Mark 3) oven.

When the kofta are cooked, carefully slit open one side of each pitta bread to make a pocket. Fill with a quarter of the carrot salad and one hot kofta.

Suggested accompaniment: yogurt, spooned into the pitta.

Citrus Satay

Serves 4

Working
(and total)
time: about
45 minutes

Calories
220

Protein
24g

Cholesterol
85mg

Total fat
12g

Saturated fat
4g

Sodium
400mg

350 g	lean leg or neck end of pork, minced	**12 oz**	**¼ tsp**	tamarind concentrate (optional)	**¼ tsp**
150 g	prawns, shelled and deveined	**5 oz**	**2 tsp**	safflower oil	**2 tsp**
1	garlic clove	**1**		**Peanut-Yogurt Satay Sauce**	
1 cm	piece fresh ginger root	**½ inch**	**45 g**	shelled peanuts, toasted, skins removed	**1½ oz**
½ tsp	fresh lime juice	**½ tsp**	**½ tsp**	grated lime rind	**½ tsp**
½ tsp	arrowroot	**½ tsp**	**1 tsp**	fresh lime juice	**1 tsp**
¾ tsp	salt	**¾ tsp**	**½ tsp**	dark brown sugar	**½ tsp**
2 tbsp	chopped fresh coriander	**2 tbsp**	**1½ tsp**	low-sodium soy sauce or shoyu	**1½ tsp**
½ tsp	ground galangal	**½ tsp**	**⅛ tsp**	salt	**⅛ tsp**
½ tsp	ground lemon grass	**½ tsp**	**4 tbsp**	plain low-fat yogurt	**4 tbsp**
¼ tsp	ground dried lemon rind (optional)	**¼ tsp**	**⅛ tsp**	chili powder	**⅛ tsp**

In a mortar, pound the prawns with the garlic, ginger, lime juice and arrowroot. Chill.

Combine the pork with the salt, coriander, galangal and lemon grass, and the lemon rind and tamarind if using. Form the mixture into eight flat, oval patties. Spoon an eighth of the prawn mixture into the middle of each patty, then mould the pork round the filling to enclose it completely. Chill the patties if you are not cooking them immediately.

Preheat the grill. Insert a wooden satay stick or metal skewer through each patty. Brush a grill pan lightly with a little of the oil, arrange the patties in the pan and brush their tips with a little more oil. Cook them under medium heat, turning once, until golden-brown on both sides – about 10 minutes.

Meanwhile, make the sauce. Grind the nuts finely in a food processor, and add the lime rind and juice, sugar, soy sauce and salt. Beat in the yogurt and add the chili powder. Serve the sauce in a bowl.

Broad Bean Pork

Serves 4		
Working time: about 30 minutes		
Total time: about 1 hour and 20 minutes		

Calories 280
Protein 33g
Cholesterol 70mg
Total fat 14g
Saturated fat 4g
Sodium 125mg

500 g	boned pork loin, trimmed of fat	**1 lb**
	freshly ground black pepper	
125 g	cooked shelled young broad beans	**4 oz**
1 tbsp	thick Greek yogurt	**1 tbsp**

1 tsp	chopped fresh summer savory	**1 tsp**
1 tsp	fresh lemon juice	**1 tsp**
8 cl	dry white wine	**3 fl oz**
17.5 cl	unsalted veal stock	**6 fl oz**

Preheat the oven to 180°C (350°F or Mark 4). Season the inside of the pork loin with a little freshly ground black pepper.

Purée the broad beans with the yogurt in a food processor , then pass the purée through a non-metallic sieve. Stir in the summer savory, add the lemon juice, and spread the mixture over the inside of the pork. Roll the pork up, lay a strip of foil over the exposed stuffing and tie it into shape with string.

Heat a heavy roasting tin or fireproof casserole, add the pork and cook over fairly high heat, turning the pork so that it browns evenly – about 5 minutes. Then transfer the casserole to the oven and cook until the pork is done – about 50 minutes.

Transfer the pork to a warmed plate, cover and leave to rest in a warm place. Stir the wine into the roasting tin and boil until almost completely evaporated. Stir in the stock and boil again until very slightly thickened. Taste, and add freshly ground black pepper and a little more lemon juice, if you wish. Carve the pork into slices, removing the foil and string, and spoon the sauce round each serving.

Suggested accompaniment: green noodles.

Pot-Roast Loin with Cherry Tomatoes

Serves 6

Working time: about 20 minutes

Total time: about 1 hour and 20 minutes

Calories 260

Protein 30g

Cholesterol 70mg

Total fat 13g

Saturated fat 4g

Sodium 90mg

750 g	boned pork loin, trimmed of fat	**1½ lb**
1 tbsp	virgin olive oil	**1 tbsp**
2 tsp	fennel seeds	**2 tsp**
1 tsp	green peppercorns	**1 tsp**
2 tbsp	white wine vinegar	**2 tbsp**
2 tbsp	white wine	**2 tbsp**
¼ tsp	salt	**¼ tsp**
250 g	cherry tomatoes, skinned	**8 oz**

Heat the oil in a fireproof casserole that just fits the pork loin then, over medium heat, lightly brown the meat all over – about 6 minutes. Pour away the oil and add the fennel seeds, peppercorns, vinegar, wine and salt to the casserole. Cover and cook gently over low heat for 1 hour; check the level of the liquid occasionally, and add more vinegar and wine if necessary. About 10 minutes before the end of cooking, add the cherry tomatoes to the casserole.

Carefully remove the meat from the casserole and cut it into 5 mm (¼ inch) thick slices. Overlap the slices down the middle of a warmed serving dish and arrange the cherry tomatoes on either side. Skim off any fat from the juices in the casserole, then pour the juices over the meat together with the fennel seeds and green peppercorns.

Roast Fillet with Pineapple Coulis

Serves 6

Working
time: about
30 minutes

Total time:
about
50 minutes

Calories
165

Protein
20g

Cholesterol
70mg

Total fat
7g

Saturated fat
3g

Sodium
140mg

750 g	pork fillet, trimmed of fat	1½ lb	1	pineapple	1
¼ tsp	salt	¼ tsp		coriander leaves, finely chopped	
	freshly ground black pepper				

Preheat the oven to 180°C (350°F or Mark 4).

Season the fillet with the salt and a little freshly ground pepper, then wrap it in lightly greased aluminium foil. Place the fillet in an ovenproof casserole or roasting tin and cook it in the oven for 35 to 45 minutes, or until the juices run clear.

While the meat cooks, peel and core the pineapple. Liquidize the pulp in a food processor or blender, then pass it through a sieve. Refrigerate the pineapple coulis until you are ready to use it.

When the meat is cooked, unwrap it and add about a tablespoon of the juices collected in the foil to the pineapple coulis. Carve the meat into slices. Spread one or two spoonfuls of coulis on each serving plate and arrange the slices of meat round it. Sprinkle with the chopped coriander.

Grape Pork

Serves 8

Working
time: about
45 minutes

Total time:
about
2 hours and
15 minutes

Calories
245
Protein
22g
Cholesterol
80mg
Total fat
8g
Saturated fat
2g
Sodium
315mg

1 kg	boned leg of pork, fillet end, trimmed of fat	**2 lb**	**¼ tsp**	ground allspice	**¼ tsp**
750 g	green grapes, halved and seeded, or small seedless green grapes	**1½ lb**	**2 tsp**	Worcester sauce	**2 tsp**
1 tsp	virgin olive oil	**1 tsp**	**½**	beaten egg	**½**
½	onion, finely chopped	**½**	**1 tsp**	salt	**1 tsp**
1	small garlic clove, crushed	**1**		freshly ground black pepper	
125 g	fine fresh breadcrumbs	**4 oz**	**1 tbsp**	arrowroot	**1 tbsp**
			12.5 cl	dry Madeira	**4 fl oz**

Preheat the oven to 180°C (350°F or Mark 4). Lay out the pork with its inner side facing up and cut in it six slits about 4 cm (1½ inches) deep. Purée 500 g (1 lb) of the grapes in a processor; sieve to strain the juice.

Heat the oil in a small frying pan and add the onion, garlic and 2 tbsp of the grape juice. Cook over medium-low heat for 5 to 7 minutes or until the onion is softened, stirring occasionally. Tip the onion into a bowl, add the breadcrumbs, allspice, Worcester sauce, egg, ½ tsp of the salt and some pepper. Add another 2 tbsp of the grape juice and mix to a soft, paste-like mixture.

Spread the paste over the pork, pushing some into the slits. Quarter about eight of the remaining grapes

and press into the stuffing. Reshape and tie securely in a rolled shape. Put into a roasting bag and place in a roasting tin. Pour the remaining grape juice round the joint and tie the bag loosely closed. Make six 1 cm (½ inch) slits in the top of the bag, then roast for 1½ hours.

Cut open the bag and lift out the pork on to a carving board. Cover and keep it warm.

Strain the juices from the roasting bag into a saucepan. Add the arrowroot, dissolved in the Madeira. Bring to the boil, stirring, and simmer until thickened. Add the remaining grapes and salt, and some pepper, and heat through for 2 to 3 minutes. Carve the pork into thin slices and serve with the sauce.

Eastern Scented Fillet

Serves 4

Working time: about 30 minutes

Total time: about 1 hour and 20 minutes

Calories 260

Protein 23g

Cholesterol 60mg

Total fat 9g

Saturated fat 3g

Sodium 185mg

400 g	pork fillet, trimmed of fat	**14 oz**
¼ tsp	salt	**¼ tsp**
½	cinnamon stick	**½**
2 tbsp	orange-flower water	**2 tbsp**
90 g	couscous	**3 oz**
60 g	dried apricots, soaked in hot water for 20 minutes	**2 oz**
30 g	raisins	**1 oz**
15 g	pine-nuts, lightly roasted	**½ oz**
½ tsp	ground coriander	**½ tsp**
¼ tsp	ground cumin	**¼ tsp**
1 tbsp	chopped fresh mint	**1 tbsp**
2 tbsp	chopped fresh tarragon	**2 tbsp**
	white pepper (optional)	
1 tsp	safflower oil	**1 tsp**
2 tsp	honey (preferably flower-scented)	**2 tsp**

Slit the fillet lengthwise with a sharp knife to a depth of half its thickness, and flatten it out as far as possible by beating with a mallet. Season the cut surface with half of the salt.

Bring ¼ litre (8 fl oz) of water to the boil with the cinnamon and orange-flower water. Add the couscous; stir for half a minute, cover tightly and remove from the heat. After 10 minutes the couscous will have absorbed all the liquid.

Drain the apricots and chop roughly; combine in a bowl with the raisins and pine-nuts. Remove the cinnamon and mix the couscous with the apricot mixture. Add the coriander, cumin, mint and tarragon; season. Stuff the fillet with this mixture, reserving any

excess for serving separately. Close up the fillet and tie round its circumference in six to eight places with string.

Preheat the oven to 190°C (375°F or Mark 5). Heat the oil in a wide, heavy or preferably non-stick frying pan over medium heat, and brown the fillet all over, starting seam side down to seal the opening. Once the fillet is brown – 5 to 10 minutes – brush it all over with the honey and wrap it fairly tight in foil. Roast the wrapped fillet for 20 minutes, then remove it from the oven and allow to rest for 5 minutes.

Open the foil and drain off the juices into a pan. Reduce the juices to a glaze and coat the fillet. Remove to a hot platter, slice and serve.

Sesame Schnitzels

Serves 4

Working time: about 20 minutes

Total time: about 30 minutes

Calories 420

Protein 31g

Cholesterol 60mg

Total fat 21g

Saturated fat 3g

Sodium 470mg

2	pork fillets (175 to 200 g/6 to 7 oz each)	2
⅛ tsp	salt	⅛ tsp
	freshly ground black pepper	
2	egg whites	2
150 g	dry granary breadcrumbs	5 oz

90 g	sesame seeds	3 oz
½ tsp	virgin olive oil	½ tsp
8	lemon slices, for garnish	8
12	fresh cranberries, cooked for 3 to 4 minutes in 1 tbsp water with 1 tbsp sugar, for garnish (optional)	12

Place a baking sheet in the oven and preheat the oven to 220°C (425°F or Mark 7). Trim off the tapered end of each piece of fillet and remove all visible fat and membrane. Cut each cylinder of meat into four rounds, then beat out the rounds to make eight escalopes. Sprinkle the meat on both sides with the salt and some pepper.

Put the egg whites in a shallow dish and whisk with a fork until they are lightly frothy. Mix the breadcrumbs and sesame seeds together and spread them out on a flat plate. Dip the pork escalopes one piece at a time in the egg whites, then coat them in the breadcrumb and sesame

seed mixture, pressing it firmly on to the meat with your hands.

Brush the heated baking sheet with the olive oil and place the meat on it. Cook the schnitzels in the oven for 10 minutes until the surfaces are golden and crisp, turning once and pressing them hard with a fish slice to keep them flat.

Arrange the schnitzels on a warmed serving platter and garnish with the lemon slices and cranberries, if you are using them.

Suggested accompaniment: colourful mixed salad with a lemon-flavoured dressing.

Cretan Roast Pork

Serves 6

Working time: about 15 minutes

Total time: about 1 hour and 15 minutes

Calories 190

Protein 21g

Cholesterol 70mg

Total fat 9g

Saturated fat 3g

Sodium 335mg

750 g	boned pork loin, trimmed of fat, rolled and tied	**1½ lb**
1 tbsp	finely chopped fresh oregano, or ½ tsp dried oregano	**1 tbsp**
1 tsp	salt	**1 tsp**
	freshly ground black pepper	
1 tbsp	virgin olive oil	**1 tbsp**
2	garlic cloves, finely chopped	**2**
250 g	plum or rather ripe tomatoes, skinned, seeded and coarsely chopped	**8 oz**
12.5 cl	red wine	**4 fl oz**
2 tbsp	fresh lemon juice	**2 tbsp**

Preheat the oven to 200°C (400°F or Mark 6). Rub the surface of the joint with the oregano, salt and some pepper. Heat the oil in a wide, shallow fireproof dish over high heat and sear the joint briefly on all sides. Cook the garlic in the oil round the joint for a few seconds, then add the tomatoes, wine and lemon juice.

Bake, uncovered, for 1 hour, turning and basting the meat from time to time with the juices. Also check occasionally to make sure the tomato mixture does not burn, adding water if necessary.

Remove the joint to a large serving dish and coat it with the thick tomato paste before carving into slices. If any paste remains, serve it as an accompaniment.

Suggested accompaniment: steamed French beans.

Lemon Pork

Calories 250

Protein 33g

Cholesterol 70mg

Total fat 11g

Saturated fat 4g

Sodium 85mg

500 g	boned pork loin, trimmed of fat	**1 lb**	
1	lemon	**1**	
	white pepper		
30 g	basil leaves	**1 oz**	
1	garlic clove, crushed	**1**	
3 tbsp	dry white wine	**3 tbsp**	

Using a potato peeler, remove the rind from the lemon in long strips, working from top to bottom. Put the lemon strips into a pan of cold water, bring it to the boil, then drain and refresh the rind under cold running water. Drain well.

Cut the strips into threads that can be inserted into a larding needle. Weave some of the threads into the outer surface of the pork, then press the remainder of the threads on to the inner surface. Season the pork inside and out with a little white pepper. Roll up the pork and secure the string.

Squeeze the juice from the lemon. Tear the basil leaves into small pieces and place in a non-reactive dish with the garlic. Place the pork on top, pour the lemon juice over, cover and leave in a cool place, turning the pork occasionally, for 4 hours.

Heat the oven to 180°C (350°F or Mark 4). Lift the pork from the marinade and place on a large piece of aluminium foil. Fold the sides of the foil up, then pour in the marinade and the wine. Fold the foil loosely over the pork and seal the edges together firmly. Place the parcel on a baking sheet in the oven until the pork is tender – about 40 minutes.

Transfer the pork to a warmed plate, cover and leave to rest. In a saucepan, boil the cooking juices until slightly thickened.

Carve the pork into slices, divide them among four warmed plates and spoon the juices round the meat.

Suggested accompaniment: steamed sliced courgettes.

Oriental Pot Roast

Serves 12

Working time: about 30 minutes

Total time: about 2 hours and 45 minutes

Calories 220

Protein 32g

Cholesterol 70mg

Total fat 8g

Saturated fat 3g

Sodium 310mg

1.5 kg	prime leg, boned loin, or other lean roasting joint, trimmed of fat and tied into shape	**3 lb**
1 tbsp	safflower oil	**1 tbsp**
2 tbsp	very finely chopped fresh ginger root	**2 tbsp**
2 tbsp	very finely chopped garlic	**2 tbsp**
1 tbsp	very finely chopped fresh green chili pepper	**1 tbsp**

4 tbsp	rice wine or dry sherry	**4 tbsp**
2 tsp	brown sugar	**2 tsp**
4 tbsp	low-sodium soy sauce or shoyu	**4 tbsp**
2	sweet red peppers, each cut into 12 strips	**2**
24	baby sweetcorn	**24**
24	small spring onions	**24**

Brown the neatly tied joint well on all sides in a very hot, dry wok or heavy frying pan. It may seem to stick at first , but if you leave the 'stuck' surface for a few seconds and the heat is high enough, the meat will soon loosen. Keep the wok unwashed for use later.

Heat the oil in a heavy-bottomed saucepan, then add the ginger, garlic and chili pepper. Stir until the paste begins to brown, then add the rice wine or sherry and bring to the boil. Reduce the heat. Stir in the sugar and soy sauce, then place the browned joint in the casserole and coat it in the mixture. Ensure the heat is very low, cover the pot and simmer for 2¼ hours.

About 15 minutes before serving, stir-fry first the red pepper strips, then the baby sweetcorn and finally the spring onions in the wok or frying pan over fierce heat. Remove each batch to a bowl after stir-frying. All the vegetables should have softened slightly and be flecked with black, but still crisp.

When the meat is ready, slice into 12 portions. Lay on a serving platter. If the liquid in the casserole has not reduced to a dark, glossy syrup, skim off any surface fat and reduce the liquid over high heat. Toss the vegetables in this syrup and make sure they are thoroughly heated through, then spoon them over the pork and serve immediately.

Fillet Persillé with Carrot Purée

Serves 4

Working time: about 40 minutes

Total time: about 50 minutes

Calories 230
Protein 22g
Cholesterol 75mg
Total fat 9g
Saturated fat 4g
Sodium 380mg

500 g	pork fillet, trimmed of fat	1 lb
½ tsp	salt	½ tsp
	freshly ground black pepper	
2 tbsp	Dijon mustard	2 tbsp
4 tbsp	finely chopped parsley	4 tbsp
30 g	fine dry white breadcrumbs	1 oz

	Carrot Purée	
350 g	carrots	12 oz
4 tbsp	fresh orange juice	4 tbsp
7 g	unsalted butter, chilled and cut into tiny cubes	¼ oz

Preheat the oven to 200°C (400°F or Mark 6). Wipe the fillet dry and season it with the salt and some pepper. Sear it in a hot, dry non-stick frying pan until it is brown all over. Brush the fillet with the mustard and sprinkle with the parsley on all sides, then carefully roll it in the breadcrumbs so it is evenly coated. Place on a wire rack over a baking tin and roast for 30 to 40 minutes, until the meat is cooked and the crumbs are brown.

Steam the carrots until tender, then purée them with the orange juice, either in a food processor or by passing them through a sieve. Heat the purée through slowly in a small pan,

gradually beating in the butter.

Let the cooked fillet rest for 10 minutes, then carve it into thick slices and serve with the carrot purée.

Suggested accompaniments: new potatoes; French beans.

Editor's Note: The fillet may also be eaten cold, cut into thin slices and served with a vinaigrette made with 2 tablespoons finely chopped carrot, 3 tablespoons each white wine vinegar and fresh orange juice, and 4 tablespoons safflower oil.

Loin Cooked in Milk

500 g	boned pork loin, trimmed of fat, rolled and tied	**1 lb**	**1**	parsley sprig	**1**
1	onion, finely chopped	**1**	**¼ tsp**	salt	**¼ tsp**
3 tbsp	unsalted veal stock or water	**3 tbsp**		freshly ground black pepper	
2	fresh bay leaves, broken	**2**	**35 cl**	skimmed milk	**12 fl oz**
1	small thyme sprig, or ¼ tsp dried thyme	**1**			

In a heavy-bottomed saucepan or fireproof casserole, gently simmer the onion in the stock or water until it is soft and the liquid evaporated – 3 to 4 minutes. Add the bay leaves, thyme and parsley. Place the pork on top, season with the salt and some pepper, then gradually pour in the milk. Increase the heat and bring the liquid to the boil, then simmer, covered, for 45 minutes to 1 hour, until the pork is just tender and the milk well reduced – a skin should form on the surface.

Lift the pork out carefully with a slotted spoon and keep it warm. Continue to simmer the sauce, if necessary, until only about 6 tablespoons remain.

Carve the pork into slices and divide it among four warmed plates. Remove the herbs from the sauce and spoon a quarter of the sauce on to each plate.

Suggested accompaniment: new potatoes with parsley.

Red Cabbage Pork

Serves 4

Working
time: about
30 minutes

Total time:
about
2 hours

Calories
310
Protein
37g
Cholesterol
110mg
Total fat
13g
Saturated fat
4g
Sodium
170mg

750 g	boned pork loin	**1½ lb**	**3**	cloves	**3**
1 tbsp	safflower oil	**1 tbsp**	**1 tsp**	sugar	**1 tsp**
1	onion, finely chopped	**1**	**3 tbsp**	fresh lemon juice	**3 tbsp**
500 g	red cabbage, shredded	**1 lb**	**2**	strips lemon rind, each about	**2**
350 g	firm pears, peeled and thickly sliced	**12 oz**		5 cm (2 inches) long	

Preheat the oven to 170°C (325°F or Mark 3). Trim the loin of all visible fat and roll it, tying it with string in several places. Heat the oil in a heavy fireproof casserole over high heat, add the pork and cook for about 3 minutes, turning the pork so that it browns evenly. Transfer the meat to a plate and set it aside.

Reduce the heat, add the onion to the casserole and cook, stirring frequently and scraping up the caramelized juices from the base of the casserole, until softened – 3 to 4 minutes. Add the cabbage in batches and cook, stirring frequently, for about 2 minutes per batch. Remove each batch to a plate before frying the next one.

Mix the cabbage and onion, pears, cloves and sugar together in a bowl, then make a thick bed of about half of the cabbage mixture in the bottom of the casserole. Add the lemon juice and strips of lemon rind. Place the pork on top and pack the remaining cabbage mixture round the meat and over the top. Cover the casserole and cook in the oven for about 1 hour and 20 minutes.

Transfer the pork to a warmed plate, cover and leave to rest. Spoon off the juices from the cabbage and boil until slightly reduced. Carve the pork into slices and divide among four warmed plates. Add the cabbage and pear mixture and spoon the juices over.

Mango Pork

Serves 8

Working time: about 35 minutes

Total time: about 2 hours and 15 minutes

Calories 270
Protein 33g
Cholesterol 70mg
Total fat 13g
Saturated fat 4g
Sodium 115mg

1 kg	boned pork loin, trimmed of fat, rolled and tied	**2 lb**
1 tbsp	virgin olive oil	**1 tbsp**
½	onion, finely chopped	**½**
1	carrot, chopped	**1**
1	stick celery, chopped	**1**
1	garlic clove, finely chopped	**1**
1 tbsp	chopped fresh ginger root	**1 tbsp**
1 tbsp	coriander seeds	**1 tbsp**
12	cardamom pods, lightly crushed to open	**12**
1 tsp	cumin seeds	**1 tsp**
½ tsp	black peppercorns	**½ tsp**
½	cinnamon stick	**½**
1	dried chili pepper, halved	**1**
30.cl	unsalted chicken stock	**½ pint**
15 cl	dry sherry	**¼ pint**
1	ripe mango, peeled, stoned and chopped	**1**
½	lemon, juice only (optional)	**½**
½	cucumber, halved lengthwise and thinly sliced, for garnish	**½**
15 g	coriander sprigs, stalks removed, leaves torn into small pieces, for garnish	**½ oz**

Preheat the oven to 180°C (350°F or Mark 4). Heat the oil in a casserole over medium-low heat. Add the vegetables, garlic and ginger. Cover and cook gently until softened – 5 to 7 mins.

Add the coriander, cardamom, cumin, peppercorns, cinnamon and chili; stir. Place the pork on top. Pour in the stock and sherry and bring to boil, cover tightly and transfer to oven. Braise for 1½ hours.

Remove pork and scrape clean. Wrap in foil and set aside.

Strain the cooking liquid into a pan, pressing down on the vegetables and spices in the sieve; discard contents of the sieve. Purée the mango with half of the strained liquid. Press through a sieve into the pan containing the remaining cooking liquid and stir. Add the lemon juice, gently reheat.

Slice the pork thinly and serve with the sauce, and cucumber and coriander garnish.

Loin Chops with Mushrooms and Sherry

<table>
<tr><td>Serves 4</td></tr>
<tr><td>Working time: about 35 minutes</td></tr>
<tr><td>Total time: about 1 hour and 20 minutes</td></tr>
</table>

Calories	270
Protein	36g
Cholesterol	70mg
Total fat	12g
Saturated fat	5g
Sodium	300mg

4	loin chops (125 g to 150 g/4½ to 5 oz each), trimmed of fat	**4**
½ tsp	salt	**½ tsp**
	freshly ground black pepper	
1	onion, finely chopped	**1**
1	garlic clove, very finely chopped	**1**
500 g	button mushrooms, finely chopped	**1 lb**
8 cl	dry sherry	**3 fl oz**
2	large sorrel leaves, deveined, cut into thin strips	**2**
75 g	fromage frais	**2½ oz**

Season the chops with the salt and a little pepper, then brown them well on both sides in a non-stick frying pan. Remove them to a heavy, fireproof casserole.

Sweat the onion and garlic, covered, in the frying pan until they are soft but not coloured. Add them to the chops in the casserole.

Put the mushrooms into the frying pan, turn up the heat and stir as they begin to cook. When they have given up their juice, add the sherry and boil vigorously for 2 minutes. Transfer them to the casserole.

Bring the contents of the casserole to the boil, then reduce the heat, cover, and leave to cook at a lively simmer for 45 minutes or until the chops are tender. Remove the chops, scraping off and returning any pieces of vegetable to the casserole, and keep warm.

Increase the heat under the mushroom mixture, and boil to reduce the liquid completely. Stir in the sorrel leaves, then remove the casserole from the heat and stir in the *fromage frais*. Serve the chops immediately on individual plates, with a large spoonful of the mushroom mixture on the top of each chop.

Suggested accompaniment: steamed broccoli.

Editor's Note: If sorrel is not available, substitute spinach and stir in 1 teaspoon of lemon juice with the *fromage frais.*

Pork Cooked Like Game

Serves 4

Working time: about 30 minutes

Total time: about 1 day (includes marinating)

Calories
220

Protein
22g

Cholesterol
70mg

Total fat
7g

Saturated fat
3g

Sodium
115mg

500 g	boned pork loin, trimmed of fat and rolled	**1 lb**
30 g	dried ceps	**1 oz**
1	onion, sliced	**1**
	Juniper Marinade	
1	small onion, finely chopped	**1**
1	small carrot, diced	**1**

10	juniper berries	**10**
4	black peppercorns, lightly crushed	**4**
1	fresh bay leaf, broken in half	**1**
1	small rosemary sprig	**1**
1	thyme sprig	**1**
1	parsley sprig	**1**
30 cl	red wine	**½ pint**

To prepare the marinade, scatter the onion and carrot in the bottom of a dish. Lay the pork on top, add juniper berries, peppercorns, bay leaf, rosemary, thyme and parsley, pour the wine over. Cover the dish and leave in a cool place for about 24 hours, turning the pork occasionally.

Pour 30 cl (½ pint) of boiling water over the mushrooms and leave to soak for 20 minutes. Strain the mushrooms and reserve the liquid.

Preheat the oven to 170°C (325°F or Mark 3). Lift the pork from the marinade; reserve the marinade. Heat a heavy casserole; add the pork and cook over high heat, turning the pork so that it browns evenly all over. Transfer to a plate.

Add the onion to the casserole and cook over low heat, stirring and scraping the caramelized meat juices from the casserole, until lightly softened – 2 to 3 minutes. Return the pork, add the mushrooms, pour over the mushroom liquid and the marinade so the pork is almost covered. Increase heat and bring to simmering point.

Cover the casserole tightly, transfer it to the oven, and cook for 40 to 45 minutes. When the meat is cooked, transfer it to a warmed plate, cover and leave to rest in a low oven.

Strain the liquid; discard bay leaf and herb sprigs but reserve vegetables. Skim off any fat from the liquid, reduce by about three quarters.

Carve the pork into slices. Serve with the reserved vegetables and reduced sauce.

Chops with Spiced Orange Sauce

Serves 4

Working time: about 20 minutes

Total time: about 35 minutes

Calories 200

Protein 21g

Cholesterol 70mg

Total fat 8g

Saturated fat 3g

Sodium 275mg

4	boneless pork loin chops (about 125 g/4 oz each), trimmed of fat	4
2	shallots, finely chopped	2
1	small sweet green pepper, seeded, deribbed and cut into thin strips	1
¼ tsp	ground cinnamon	¼ tsp
⅛ tsp	ground cloves	⅛ tsp
3	large oranges, juice and grated rind of two, one peeled and thinly sliced	3
1 tbsp	soft brown sugar	1 tbsp
2 tsp	arrowroot	2 tsp
½ tsp	salt	½ tsp
	freshly ground black pepper	

In a large non-stick frying pan, brown the chops over high heat for 3 minutes, turning once. Add the shallots and green pepper and continue to cook, stirring, for 2 minutes. Stir in the cinnamon and cloves.

Put the orange juice into a measuring jug and make the liquid up to ¼ litre (8 fl oz) with water. Add the liquid to the pan together with the orange rind and sugar. Bring to the boil, then reduce the heat and simmer for about 10 minutes,

until the chops are tender.

Using a slotted spoon, remove the pork chops to a serving plate and keep warm. Add the orange slices to the pan and heat through.

In a small bowl or cup, mix the arrowroot with 2 tablespoons of cold water, then add to the pan and stir well until the sauce thickens. Season with the salt and some freshly ground pepper. Spoon the orange sauce round the pork to serve.

Light Gumbo

Serves 4

Working time: about 30 minutes

Total time: about 2 hours

Calories 290

Protein 40g

Cholesterol 145mg

Total fat 13g

Saturated fat 5g

Sodium 370mg

350 g	lean pork, trimmed of fat and cut into 1 cm ($\frac{1}{2}$ inch) cubes	**12 oz**
250 g	cooked prawns, unpeeled	**8 oz**
3	parsley sprigs	**3**
$\frac{1}{2}$ tsp	black peppercorns	**$\frac{1}{2}$ tsp**
$\frac{1}{2}$ tsp	salt	**$\frac{1}{2}$ tsp**
1	onion, finely chopped	**1**
1	garlic clove, crushed	**1**
250 g	okra, trimmed and cut into 2.5 cm (1 inch) slices	**8 oz**

1	fresh green chili pepper, finely chopped	**1**
250 g	tomatoes, skinned, seeded and cut into fine strips	**8 oz**
3 tbsp	finely chopped fresh coriander, or 3 tbsp chopped parsley plus 2 tbsp fresh lime juice	**3 tbsp**

Remove the heads and shells from the prawns and set the flesh aside. Bring the heads and shells to the boil in 1 litre (1$\frac{3}{4}$ pints) of water with the parsley sprigs and peppercorns, cover and simmer for 20 minutes. Strain the prawn stock through a sieve and set aside; discard the solids.

Brown the meat in a dry non-stick frying pan, stir in the salt, then add the onion and garlic and cook for about 5 minutes, until the onion has softened. Transfer the contents of the frying pan to a saucepan, add the stock and bring to the boil. Cover and leave to simmer until the meat is very tender – about 1$\frac{1}{2}$ hours.

Toss the okra in a wok or dry non-stick frying pan over high heat until it is charred in places but still green and crisp. Stir in the chili pepper and cook briefly, then tip the mixture into the stew. Add the tomatoes, coriander, or parsley and lime juice, and the prawns. Bring the stew quickly to the boil and serve.

Suggested accompaniment: crusty bread or boiled rice.

Editor's Note: Gumbo is usually served in bowls as a soup-stew and eaten with spoons.

Pork Stroganoff

Serves 4

Working
(and total)
time: about
25 minutes

Calories
250

Protein
24g

Cholesterol
70mg

Total fat
14g

Saturated fat
4g

Sodium
190mg

500 g	pork fillet, trimmed of fat and cut into thin strips	**1 lb**
1½ tbsp	safflower oil	**1½ tbsp**
1	large onion, quartered, thinly sliced	**1**
175 g	button mushrooms, sliced	**6 oz**
2 tbsp	plain wholemeal flour	**2 tbsp**
30 cl	unsalted chicken stock	**½ pint**
1 tbsp	tomato paste	**1 tbsp**
1 tsp	fresh lemon juice	**1 tsp**
¼ tsp	salt	**¼ tsp**
	freshly ground black pepper	
60 g	thick Greek yogurt	**2 oz**

Heat the oil in a large frying pan until it is smoking, add the pork strips and onion and cook for 3 minutes, stirring frequently, until the pork is browned all over. Add the mushrooms and cook for a further minute, stirring.

Add the flour to the pan and mix well, then gradually stir in the stock and bring to the boil, stirring all the time. Reduce the heat and simmer for 2 minutes, then stir in the tomato paste, lemon juice, salt and some pepper. Heat the mixture through gently for 2 minutes.

Remove the pan from the heat, stir in the yogurt and serve immediately.

Suggested accompaniment: green or wholewheat tagliatelle.

Portuguese Pork

Serves 4

Working time: about 30 minutes

Total time: about 1 hour and 15 minutes

Calories
350

Protein
28g

Cholesterol
70mg

Total fat
14g

Saturated fat
4g

Sodium
135mg

500 g	pork fillet, trimmed of fat, thickly sliced	**1 lb**
1 tbsp	safflower oil	**1 tbsp**
1	large onion, thinly sliced	**1**
2	garlic cloves, crushed	**2**
750 g	plum tomatoes, quartered, or 400 g (14 oz) canned tomatoes, drained	**3 tbsp**
2 tbsp	tomato paste	**2 tbsp**
15 cl	dry white wine	**¼ pint**

15 cl	unsalted vegetable or chicken stock	**¼ pint**
2 tbsp	chopped parsley	**2 tbsp**
2 tbsp	chopped fresh basil	**2 tbsp**
1 tsp	dried mixed herbs	**1 tsp**
½ tsp	sugar	**½ tsp**
⅛ tsp	salt	**⅛ tsp**
	freshly ground black pepper	
250 g	fresh or frozen peas	**8 oz**
1	sweet yellow pepper, seeded, deribbed and thinly sliced lengthwise	**1**

Heat the safflower oil in a heavy fireproof casserole, add the sliced onion and cook gently, stirring, until it is soft and lightly coloured – about 5 minutes. Stir in the crushed garlic, tomatoes, tomato paste, white wine and stock. Bring to the boil, stirring, then reduce the heat and add half of the chopped parsley and basil, the dried mixed herbs, sugar, salt and some pepper. Simmer, uncovered, stirring occasionally, for about 20 minutes, until the sauce is reduced and quite thick.

Meanwhile, brown the slices of pork in batches in a hot non-stick frying pan over medium-high heat, then drain them on paper towels.

Add the pork to the casserole, cover, reduce the heat and simmer for 25 minutes, stirring occasionally, until the meat is tender. If you are using fresh peas, add these to the casserole after 5 minutes. Add the sliced yellow pepper after 20 minutes, together with the frozen peas, if using. Just before serving, stir in the remaining chopped parsley and basil.

Pork Vindaloo

Serves 8

Working
time: about
15 minutes

Total time:
about
26 hours
(includes
marinating)

Calories
200
Protein
22g
Cholesterol
70mg
Total fat
10g
Saturated fat
3g
Sodium
265mg

1 kg	lean leg or neck end of pork, trimmed and cut into small cubes	**2 lb**
300 g	tomatoes, roughly chopped	**10 oz**
1	sweet green pepper, seeded and chopped	**1**
1	large onion, sliced	**1**
3	garlic cloves, crushed	**3**
1 tbsp	safflower oil	**1 tbsp**
1 tsp	cumin seeds	**1 tsp**
1 tsp	yellow mustard seeds	**1 tsp**

1 tsp	ground cinnamon	**1 tsp**
1 tsp	mustard powder	**1 tsp**
½ tsp	ground turmeric	**½ tsp**
10	black peppercorns, crushed	**10**
6	small red chili peppers, fresh or dried	**6**
6 tbsp	vinegar	**6 tbsp**
2 tbsp	plain low-fat yogurt	**2 tbsp**
½	lemon, grated rind and juice	**½**
¼ tsp	salt (optional)	**¼ tsp**
4 tbsp	chopped fresh coriander	**4 tbsp**

Heap the pork and all the other ingredients except the salt and fresh coriander in a large non-reactive bowl and mix them together well. Cover the bowl and leave to marinate for 24 hours.

Transfer the mixture to a large saucepan and simmer gently for 1½ hours, stirring occasionally and adding a little water if it appears too dry. At the end of cooking, taste a little of the stew and add the salt if required. Stir in the choped coriander before serving.

Suggested accompaniment: cinnamon creamed potatoes.

Editor's Note: This dish will taste even better if kept in the refrigerator and eaten the following day.

Pork Dopiaza

<table>
<tr><td>Serves 6</td></tr>
<tr><td>Working time: about 25 minutes</td></tr>
<tr><td>Total time: about 1 hour and 15 minutes</td></tr>
</table>

Calories	290
Protein	27g
Cholesterol	80mg
Total fat	12g
Saturated fat	4g
Sodium	250mg

750 g	lean leg or neck end of pork, trimmed of fat and cut into small cubes	1½ lb
3 tbsp	safflower oil	3 tbsp
1.5 kg	onions, 1 kg (2 lb) finely sliced, 500 g (1 lb) coarsely chopped	3 lb
300 g	tomatoes, chopped	10 oz
4	garlic cloves, crushed	4
1 tsp	ground coriander	1 tsp
1 tsp	chili powder	1 tsp
1 tsp	ground cinnamon	1 tsp

4	bay leaves	4
	ground turmeric	
5 cm	piece fresh ginger root, peeled and sliced	2 inch
8	black peppercorns, crushed	8
1 tbsp	plain low-fat yogurt	1 tbsp
½ tsp	salt	½ tsp
1	lemon, juice only	1
6	fresh coriander sprigs, torn into pieces	6

Heat half of the oil in a large frying pan and add the pork, half the sliced onions, the tomatoes, garlic, ground coriander, chili powder, cinnamon, bay leaves and about ½ teaspoon of turmeric. Toss the contents of the pan and cook for 2 minutes, stirring occasionally. Add the remaining sliced onions, cover the pan and cook gently for 1 hour or until tender.

About 15 minutes before serving, heat the remaining oil in another frying pan and add the chopped onions, ginger, peppercorns and a pinch of turmeric for colour. Cook until the onions are nearly golden, then stir in the yogurt. Transfer the onions to the pork in the first pan and add the salt and lemon juice. Serve in the pan, garnished with the fresh coriander.

Suggested accompaniment: plain boiled rice.

Pork Schpundra

Serves 4

Working
time: about
20 minutes

Total time:
about
1 hour and
20 minutes

Calories
240
Protein
25g
Cholesterol
70mg
Total fat
8g
Saturated fat
3g
Sodium
400mg

500 g	neck end or other lean stewing pork, trimmed of fat and cut into 2 cm (¾ inch) cubes	**1 lb**
1 tbsp	safflower oil	**1 tbsp**
500 g	fresh beetroot, cut into 2 cm (¾ inch) cubes	**1 lb**
1	red onion, sliced	**1**
30 cl	light beer	**½ pint**
2 tbsp	barley malt syrup	**2 tbsp**

8	black peppercorns	**8**
4	allspice berries	**4**
1	fresh or dried bay leaf	**1**
1	fresh mint sprig	**1**
½ tsp	salt	**½ tsp**
1 tbsp	potato flour, dissolved in 2 tbsp water	**1 tbsp**
125 g	smetana or thick Greek yogurt	**4 oz**

Heat the oil in a large fireproof casserole. Add the meat and brown the cubes evenly on all sides over high heat – about 1 minute. Add the beetroot, onion ,beer, malt syrup, peppercorns, allspice, bay leaf, mint and salt. Bring to the boil and simmer gently for 1 to 1¼ hours, until the meat is tender.

Add the potato flour mixture to the casserole and cook a little further to thicken the liquid, stirring all the time. Serve hot, topping each serving with a swirl of the smetana or yogurt.

Suggested accompaniment: rye bread.

Coachman's Pork

Serves 6

Working time: about 40 minutes

Total time: about 2 hours and 40 minutes

Calories 235
Protein 19g
Cholesterol 125mg
Total fat 7g
Saturated fat 3g
Sodium 280mg

500 g	pork loin or other lean pork, cut into 1 cm (½ inch) strips	**1 lb**
2 tsp	safflower oil	**2 tsp**
750 g	onions, thickly sliced	**1½ lb**
4	lamb's kidneys, quartered and trimmed	**4**
1 kg	potatoes, cut into 3 mm (⅛ inch) slices	**2 lb**
17.5 cl	lager	**6 fl oz**
30 cl	unsalted veal stock	**½ pint**
½ tsp	salt	**½ tsp**
	freshly ground black pepper	

Heat the oil in a large frying pan. Add the onions and cook over medium heat, stirring from time to time, until the onions start turning brown at the edges. Remove from the pan and set aside.

In the same pan, fry the pork strips, a few at a time, until well browned. Set them aside. Fry the kidney pieces in the pan to sear them.

Preheat the oven to 190°C (375°F or Mark 5). In the bottom of a deep ovenproof dish, spread a third of the onions, then a third of the potatoes, the kidneys, another third of the onions, another third of potatoes, the pork, a final layer of onions, then potatoes.

Over high heat, deglaze the frying pan with the lager. Boil rapidly until almost completely reduced, then add the stock, salt and some pepper, and bring back to the boil. Pour the liquid over the ingredients in the dish. Cover with foil and bake for 2 hours. Remove the foil after 1 hour, so the top can brown. Serve hot.

Suggested accompaniment: steamed winter greens.

Blanquette Anisette

Serves 4

Working
time: about
40 minutes

Total time:
about
1 hour and
40 minutes

Calories
250

Protein
25g

Cholesterol
100mg

Total fat
8g

Saturated fat
3g

Sodium
370mg

500 g	neck end, blade or other stewing pork, trimmed of fat and cut into cubes	**1 lb**
¾ litre	unsalted chicken stock	**1¼ pints**
1	fennel bulb, feathery top reserved	**1**
1	clove	**1**
1	bay leaf, fresh or dried	**1**
3	shallots, peeled and separated	**3**
100 g	white button mushrooms	**3½ oz**
15 cl	dry white wine	**¼ pint**

1–2 tbsp	fresh lemon juice	**1–2 tbsp**
200 g	white baby turnips, or larger turnips, halved or quartered	**7 oz**
½ tsp	salt	**½ tsp**
15 cl	skimmed milk	**¼ pint**
½ tsp	potato flour	**½ tsp**
1	egg yolk	**1**
4 tbsp	smetana	**4 tbsp**
1 tbsp	anise-flavoured spirit (optional)	**1 tbsp**

Cover the pork in a casserole with the stock or water. Bring to the boil slowly and skim, then add the fennel bulb – studded with the clove – the bay leaf and shallots. Simmer, skimming occasionally, for 1 hr or until the meat is nearly tender. Cook the mushrooms for 2 mins in the wine, with a dash of lemon juice. Add to the casserole with the wine, then add turnips and salt. Simmer for 20 mins.

When vegetables are tender, drain casserole contents, reserving the liquid. Discard the bay leaf, clove and shallots. Quarter the fennel.

Sieve the cooking liquid into a measuring jug. Reserve 1 tbsp of the milk, and add the rest to the cooking liquid to make up ½ litre (16 fl oz). Beat the potato flour with the reserved milk, egg yolk and smetana. Beat a little of the stock-and-milk liquid into this, then whisk the whole back into the stock. Return it to the casserole and heat, whisking, to a simmer. Add pork and vegetables and simmer until liquid coats the back of a spoon. Do not boil. Add spirit and lemon juice to taste. Garnish with fennel tops.

Fillet with Wheat Grains and Gin

Serves 4

Working time: about 20 minutes

Total time: about 10 hours (includes soaking)

Calories
280

Protein
24g

Cholesterol
60mg

Total fat
8g

Saturated fat
3g

Sodium
75mg

350 g	pork fillet, cut into strips about 6 by 1 cm (2½ by ½ inch)	**12 oz**
100 g	whole wheat grains	**3½ oz**
1	orange, peeled and divided into segments, 1 strip of rind pared and reserved	**1**
10	juniper berries, crushed	**10**
17.5 cl	fresh orange juice	**6 fl oz**
3 tbsp	dry gin	**3 tbsp**
60 g	spring onions, thinly sliced	**2 oz**
45 g	fromage frais	**1½ oz**
1 tbsp	chopped parsley	**1 tbsp**
	freshly ground black pepper	

Place the wheat grains and the orange rind in a saucepan of cold water and leave to soak overnight.

Drain the wheat grains, add them to a saucepan of boiling water and simmer for 35 to 45 minutes, or until the grains are cooked but still have bite.

While the wheat is cooking, heat the juniper berries in a small, heavy-bottomed saucepan for about 3 minutes, then add the orange juice and gin. Warm through gently, then cover, remove from the heat and leave to infuse for 30 minutes.

Heat the juniper infusion to just below simmering point. Add the pork in two or three batches and poach each batch for 2 minutes; when cooked, lift each batch from the liquid

with a slotted spoon and keep it warm. Add the spring onions to the liquid, then simmer until the liquid is reduced by one third and the spring onions are cooked. Add any juices from the pork towards the end of cooking time. Reduce the heat to very low and whisk in the *fromage frais*.

When the wheat is cooked, drain it and place it in a warmed serving bowl, discarding the orange rind.

Remove the sauce from the heat, add the pork and parsley, and season with some black pepper. Pour the sauce and pork over the wheat grains and toss lightly with the orange segments.

Fennel Pork

Serves 6

Working
(and total)
time: about
40 minutes

Calories
160

Protein
22g

Cholesterol
70mg

Total fat
7g

Saturated fat
3g

Sodium
220mg

| 6 | boneless pork steaks (about 125 g/4 oz each), trimmed of fat freshly ground black pepper | 6 |
| 300 g | fennel bulbs, feathery tops reserved | 10 oz |

35 cl	unsalted veal or chicken stock	12 fl oz
1 tbsp	anise-flavoured spirit	1 tbsp
45 g	fromage frais	1½ oz
¼ tsp	salt	¼ tsp
	white pepper	

Using a small, sharp knife, cut into the side of each steak to make a deep cavity. Season the pockets with some freshly ground black pepper.

Remove three outer leaves from each fennel bulb, and cut each leaf in half. In a large pan simmer the leaves in the stock for 5 minutes. Lift them from the stock with a slotted spoon and divide them among the cavities in the chops. Place the chops in a steamer.

Chop the remaining fennel and add it to the stock. Place the steamer over the stock and steam the steaks for 6 to 8 minutes, turning them over half way through. Remove the steamer from the pan and keep the steaks warm.

Continue to boil the fennel in the stock until it is tender – about 5 minutes – then remove it with a slotted spoon and set aside. Add the spirit to the stock and boil until the liquid has reduced to about 4 tablespoons, then put it in a food processor with the fennel and fromage frais, and purée them. Transfer the purée to a pan, add the salt and some white pepper, and warm over low heat, stirring occasionally.

Place the steaks on a warmed dish, spoon the sauce round them, and garnish with the fennel fronds.

Suggested accompaniment: green beans.

Pork Couscous

Serves 6

Working
time: about
30 minutes

Total time:
about
1 hour and
30 minutes
(includes
marinating)

Calories
400

Protein
25g

Cholesterol
80mg

Total fat
15g

Saturated fat
5g

Sodium
380mg

750 g	neck end or other lean pork, cut into 1 cm (½ inch) cubes	**1½ lb**	**6**	small carrots, or chunks of large carrots	**6**
1	onion	**1**	**350 g**	aubergines cut into 2.5 cm (1 inch) cubes	**12 oz**
1	lemon, juice only	**1**	**300 g**	small courgettes, sliced diagonally	**10 oz**
1 tsp	salt	**1 tsp**	**6**	fresh dates, stoned and halved	**6**
½ tsp	ground cinnamon	**½ tsp**	**125 g**	cooked chick-peas	**4 oz**
5 cm	piece fresh ginger root	**2 inch**	**500 g**	couscous	**1 lb**
6	small turnips, or chunks of large turnips	**6**	**1½ tbsp**	harissa	**1½ tbsp**

Purée the onion with the lemon juice, salt and cinnamon in a processor. Marinate the pork in this paste for 30 minutes.

Place the ginger in 60 cl (1 pint) of water in a pan over which you can fit a closely fitting two-tier steamer with a lid. Bring water to the boil.

Pick out the meat from the marinade, but do not scrape off the paste. Arrange in the bottom tier of the steamer with the turnips, carrots and aubergines. Cover, and steam for 30 mins.

Add the courgettes, dates and chick-peas to the meat mixture. Cover, steam for 20 minutes.

Meanwhile, put the couscous in a bowl, pour on

45 cl (¾ pint) of lukewarm water and leave to swell for 10 mins, stirring occasionally.

About 10 mins before the meat and vegetables are ready, put the couscous in the upper tier, uncovered. The couscous is done when steam penetrates its surface. If this has not happened by the time the meat and vegetables are cooked, take out the bottom tier and put the couscous directly over the saucepan.

Pile the couscous on to a serving platter. Arrange the meat and vegetables on top. Dilute the harissa with 30 cl (½ pint) of the gingery steaming liquid, and serve it separately. The remaining liquid may also be passed round to moisten the meat and vegetables.

Pork and Burghul Meatballs

Serves 6

IIII
Working
time: about
30 minutes

Total time:
about
1 hour and
10 minutes

Calories
240

Protein
27g

Cholesterol
70mg

Total fat
9g

Saturated fat
5g

Sodium
230mg

350 g	neck end or other lean pork, minced	12 oz
90 g	fine-grade burghul	3 oz
3 tbsp	very finely chopped onion	3 tbsp
¾ tsp	ground roasted cumin seed	¾ tsp
½ tsp	salt	½ tsp
	freshly ground black pepper	

4 tbsp	finely chopped parsley	4 tbsp
125 g	thick Greek yogurt	4 oz
1 tsp	arrowroot	1 tsp
1	garlic clove, finely chopped	1
½ tsp	grated lemon rind	½ tsp
	cayenne pepper	

Knead the minced pork with the burghul, onion, cumin, salt and some pepper. Let the mixture stand for 10 minutes, knead again briefly, then form into 24 balls. Roll the balls in the parsley, pressing them in so that the herb coating sticks. Arrange the balls, in a single layer, in a steamer over a saucepan of boiling water, cover and steam for 40 minutes.

Towards the end of this time, put the yogurt in a small pan. Mix the arrowroot with a little cold water, and stir into the yogurt; add the garlic, the lemon rind and a pinch of cayenne. Gradually beat in 6 tablespoons of hot water from the steaming pan and bring to the boil over medium heat, stirring constantly. When the sauce has thickened, let it sit for 5 minutes off the heat, so that the arrowroot is completely absorbed.

Bring the sauce back to the boil just before serving. Serve the meatballs directly from the steamer, accompanied by the hot sauce.

Suggested accompaniment: rice mixed with peas.

Editor's Note: A bamboo steamer will provide a wider flatter surface for the meatballs than an ordinary steamer.

Ham with Broad Beans

Serves 6

Working time: about 15 minutes

Total time: about 30 minutes

Calories 130
Protein 10g
Cholesterol 15mg
Total fat 4g
Saturated fat 2g
Sodium 390mg

175 g	lean ham, diced	**6 oz**
750 g	shelled broad beans	**1¼ lb**
1 tsp	safflower oil	**1 tsp**
1 tbsp	plain flour	**1 tbsp**
4 tbsp	white wine (optional)	**4 tbsp**

	freshly ground black pepper	
2 tbsp	single cream	**2 tbsp**
2 tbsp	finely chopped fresh summer savory, or 1½ tsp dried summer savory	**2 tbsp**

Bring a saucepan of water to the boil, add the broad beans and simmer until they are soft but still resistant – about 5 minutes. Strain them and set aside, reserving the cooking liquid.

Heat the oil in a large-bottomed saucepan; add the diced ham and fry gently for 1 minute. Stir in the flour and cook for a further minute, stirring continuously. Add the wine, if you are using it, and about 15 cl (¼ pint) of the bean cooking liquid. Simmer the mixture for 2 minutes,

adding more cooking liquid if the sauce is too thick. Season with some freshly ground black pepper. Add the cream and allow the liquid to bubble up once.

Stir the beans into the pan, warm through, sprinkle with the summer savory and serve.

Editor's Note: The skin of broad beans is rich in fibre but has a slightly bitter; if preferred, the beans may be peeled before they are cooked.

Pork and Spinach Terrine

Serves 12

Working time: about 45 minutes

Total time: about 11 hours (includes chilling)

Calories
135

Protein
16g

Cholesterol
45mg

Total fat
5g

Saturated fat
2g

Sodium
190mg

750 g	lean pork steaks, trimmed of fat	**1½ lb**
1	large onion, finely chopped	**1**
125 g	fresh wholemeal breadcrumbs	**4 oz**
2	garlic cloves, crushed	**2**
1	egg, beaten	**1**
1 tbsp	virgin olive oil	**1 tbsp**
1½ tsp	chopped fresh sage	**1½ tsp**

½ tsp	salt	**½ tsp**
	freshly ground black pepper	
150 g	boneless chicken breast, skinned	**5 oz**
1 tbsp	dry vermouth	**1 tbsp**
12	large spinach leaves, washed and stems trimmed	**12**
	lemon slices, for garnish	

Mince the pork in a processor or by hand. Put the pork into a bowl, add the onion, breadcrumbs, garlic, egg, oil, sage, half the salt and some pepper. Mix well together and set aside.

Cut the chicken into thin slices and place in a bowl with the vermouth, remaining salt and some pepper. Reserve 8 spinach leaves; finely shred the remainder, add to chicken and mix. Preheat the oven to 180°C (350°F or Mark 4).

Blanch the reserved spinach in a little boiling water in a pan for 1 minute. Drain, refresh with cold water, and drain again. Pat leaves dry on paper towels. Use the spinach leaves to line a 1 kg (2 lb) loaf tin: arrange 3 leaves, slightly overlapping, over the base and along each side,

and place the remaining leaves at either end. Allow the edges of the leaves to overlap the rim.

Press half of the pork mixture into the lined tin. Arrange the chicken over the pork, top with remaining pork mixture, press to level. Fold overlapping leaves over, cover tightly with greased foil and place the tin inside a roasting tin half-filled with cold water. Cook for 1¾ hours.

Remove tin from the oven, cover it with foil and weight down with a heavy weight placed on a board or lid that fits over the top of the terrine. Leave to cool, then chill in the refrigerator for about 8 hours. Turn out on to a serving board or platter. Pat dry with paper towels, and garnish with the lemon slices. Serve sliced.

Stuffed Chinese Cabbage Leaves

Serves 6

Working (and total) time: about 1 hour

Calories 250

Protein 27g

Cholesterol 90mg

Total fat 14g

Saturated fat 5g

Sodium 230mg

750 g	pork fillet, trimmed of fat and minced	**1½ lb**
12	Chinese cabbage leaves	**12**
1	onion, finely chopped	**1**
175 g	brown cap or oyster mushrooms, chopped	**6 oz**
2	oranges, juice and grated rind of 1½ pared, julienned rind of the other half	**2**

½ tsp	salt	**½ tsp**
	freshly ground black pepper	
½ tsp	grated nutmeg	**½ tsp**
2 tbsp	safflower oil	**2 tbsp**
1 tbsp	low-sodium soy sauce or shoyu	**1 tbsp**

Blanch the cabbage leaves in boiling water for 1 minute and drain them flat on paper towels. Sweat the onion in a heavy frying pan until transparent, then add the mushrooms and stir-fry for 4 to 5 minutes.

In a bowl, mix together the pork, onion and mushrooms, and the grated orange rind; season with the salt, some pepper and the nutmeg. Pare down the thick part of the cabbage stems with a sharp knife so the leaves will wrap easily round the stuffing. Place about 1½ tablespoons of the pork mixture on the stem end of each leaf, then roll up and tuck in the sides.

Heat the oil in the frying pan and fry the parcels, seam side down, for about 7 minutes, then turn and cook for a further 7 minutes, or until golden. Remove the cooked parcels to a serving dish. Deglaze the pan with the soy sauce and the orange juice; reduce the liquid for a minute or so, and pour it over the parcels. Garnish with the julienned orange rind and serve.

Pork Risotto

Serves 4		Calories 460
Working time: about 25 minutes		Protein 24g
		Cholesterol 55mg
Total time: about 40 minutes		Total fat 12g
		Saturated fat 4g
		Sodium 100mg

350 g	pork fillet, trimmed of fat and cut into small cubes	**12 oz**
1 tbsp	virgin olive oil	**1 tbsp**
1	onion, finely chopped	**1**
1	garlic clove, crushed	**1**
125 g	button mushrooms, roughly chopped	**4 oz**
½ tsp	chopped fresh sage	**½ tsp**
250 g	Italian round-grain rice	**8 oz**

½ tsp	salt	**½ tsp**
	freshly ground black pepper	
30 cl	dry white wine	**½ pint**
125 g	shelled peas, blanched in boiling water, or frozen peas	**4 oz**
1 tbsp	freshly grated Parmesan cheese	**1 tbsp**
3 tbsp	flat-leaf parsley, torn into small pieces	**3 tbsp**

Heat the olive oil in a heavy-bottomed saucepan over medium heat and brown the cubes of meat. Stir in the onion and continue cooking until the onion begins to turn golden at the edges. Add the garlic, mushrooms and sage. When the mushrooms are wilting, increase the heat, add the rice, salt and some pepper, and stir for a couple of minutes.

Mix the white wine with an equal amount of water and pour half of the liquid into the saucepan. Reduce the heat and stir while bringing the liquid to a gentle simmer. Stir the mixture frequently as the liquid is absorbed – 5 to 10 minutes.

Pour in the rest of the liquid and the peas, bring back to a simmer and stir. Cover the pan and leave to cook very slowly, stirring from time to time until the mixture is creamy but not mushy – 10 to 15 minutes. Just before serving, stir in the cheese and parsley.

Suggested accompaniment: tomato salad.

Pilaff with Pig's Heart

Serves 6

Working time: about 20 minutes

Total time: about 45 minutes

Calories 565
Protein 15g
Cholesterol 60mg
Total fat 15g
Saturated fat 3g
Sodium 175mg

1	pig's heart (about 250 g/8 oz), trimmed of fat and finely diced	1
2 tbsp	virgin olive oil	2 tbsp
1	onion, finely chopped	1
2 tbsp	pine-nuts	2 tbsp
350 g	long-grain rice	12 oz
2 tbsp	currants	2 tbsp

¼ tsp	sugar	¼ tsp
¼ tsp	ground allspice	¼ tsp
¼ tsp	ground cinnamon	¼ tsp
½ tsp	salt	½ tsp
	freshly ground black pepper	
3 tbsp	finely chopped parsley	3 tbsp

Heat the olive oil in a heavy-bottomed saucepan over medium heat and sauté the diced heart for about 5 minutes. Add the onion and pine-nuts, and cook until both are beginning to colour. Add the rice and stir to coat well with oil, then stir in ¾ litre (1¼ pints) of water and all the remaining ingredients except the parsley. Bring to the boil, reduce the heat, cover and simmer for 10 minutes.

Stir in the parsley, re-cover the pan and leave the pilaff to stand, off the heat, for 15 minutes more. Mix well and serve hot or warm.

Suggested accompaniments: steamed or grilled baby courgettes; grilled and skinned sweet pepper strips.

Scandinavian Gratin

Serves 6

Working time: about 30 minutes

Total time: about 2 hours

Calories 290

Protein 20g

Cholesterol 85mg

Total fat 13g

Saturated fat 4g

Sodium 365mg

250 g	pork fillet or loin, trimmed of fat and cut into thin slices	**8 oz**
500 g	potatoes, thinly sliced	**1 lb**
250 g	onions, thinly sliced	**8 oz**
350 g	fresh herring fillets	**12 oz**
1 tsp	salt	**1 tsp**
	white pepper	
15 cl	skimmed milk	**¼ pint**
1	egg yolk	**1**
125 g	smetana	**4 oz**
2	parsley sprigs, finely chopped (optional)	**2**

Preheat the oven to 220°C (425°F or Mark 7).

Lightly grease a 1.5 to 1.75 litre (2½ to 3 pint) ovenproof gratin dish. Layer the sliced potatoes, onions, herring fillets and pork slices in the dish, beginning and ending with a layer of potatoes and seasoning each layer lightly with the salt and some pepper. Pour the milk into the dish.

Place the dish in the centre of the oven and bake the gratin for 15 minutes, then reduce the heat to 190°C (375°F or Mark 5) and bake for a further hour. Check that the contents of the dish are tender by inserting a skewer in the centre of the dish – it should meet with no resistance.

Remove the dish from the oven and carefully pour out the thin juices into a bowl. Beat the egg yolk with the smetana, then beat a couple of spoonfuls of the hot cooking juices into the egg liaison. Whisk this into the remaining juices in the bowl and return the liquid to the dish.

Return to the oven for a further 15 minutes. If the top layer of potatoes is already browned, cover the dish with aluminium foil for the first 10 minutes; if the potatoes still look a little pale at end of the cooking time, brown briefly under a hot grill.

Cut the gratin into wedges and serve hot, garnished with the chopped parsley, if you are using it.

Suggested accompaniment: a colourful salad; French beans or garden peas.

Italian 'Money-Bags'

Serves 4

Working time: about 40 minutes

Total time: about 1 hour

Calories 200
Protein 22g
Cholesterol 60mg
Total fat 10g
Saturated fat 4g
Sodium 340mg

350 g	pork fillet, trimmed of fat	**12 oz**	**125 g**	sweet red pepper, seeded, deribbed and diced	**4 oz**
½ tsp	salt	**½ tsp**	**45 g**	low-fat ricotta cheese	**1½ oz**
	freshly ground black pepper		**2 tbsp**	fresh basil leaves, torn or chopped	**2 tbsp**
1	ear of sweetcorn, husked, or 125 g (4 oz) sweetcorn kernels	**1**	**1 tbsp**	fresh oregano, chopped	**1 tbsp**
250 g	broccoli	**8 oz**	**30 g**	low-fat mozzarella	**1 oz**
2 tsp	virgin olive oil	**2 tsp**			

Cut the fillet into 20 rounds and beat these out until they are almost translucent and three times their original size. Season lightly with half of the salt and some freshly ground black pepper.

Cook the sweetcorn cob in boiling water, covered, for about 7 minutes; slice off the kernels. Or, if using, briefly blanch the sweetcorn kernels.

Separate the broccoli to give at least 20 tiny florets; peel and thinly dice the stems. Blanch the broccoli briefly in boiling water and drain.

Preheat the oven to 190°C (375°F or Mark 5). Brush the base and sides of a large, shallow ovenproof dish with 1 teaspoon of the oil.

Mix all the vegetables with the ricotta and remaining salt, and add the basil and oregano.

Divide this mixture equally among the 20 pieces of fillet. Gather up the edges of each piece to enclose the filling, leaving some of the vegetable stuffing exposed to view. Divide the mozzarella into 20 tiny cubes and top each 'money-bag' with a single cube. Grind a little more black pepper on to each open parcel and arrange in the ovenproof dish. Brush remaining oil over the exposed surfaces of meat.

Bake the parcels in the centre of the oven for 15 to 20 minutes, or until the meat is cooked through and the edges are tinged brown. If you wish, brown the mozzarella a little more under a hot grill, but do not allow the pork to stiffen too much. Serve hot.

Pitta Pork Balls

Serves 6

Working
(and total)
time: about
1 hour

Calories
230

Protein
16g

Cholesterol
30mg

Total fat
6g

Saturated fat
2g

Sodium
280mg

250 g	pork loin, trimmed of fat and minced	8 oz
125 g	burghul	4 oz
2 tsp	safflower oil	2 tsp
1	onion, very finely chopped	1
1	garlic clove, crushed	1
2 tsp	curry powder	2 tsp
½ tsp	ground coriander	½ tsp
¼ tsp	ground cinnamon	¼ tsp
¼ tsp	salt	¼ tsp

6	wholemeal pitta breads	6
8	cos lettuce leaves, washed, dried and finely shredded	8
10 cm	piece cucumber, thinly sliced	4 inch
200 g	tomatoes, thinly sliced	7 oz
	Yogurt Dressing	
8 cl	plain low-fat yogurt	3 fl oz
1 tbsp	chopped fresh mint	1 tbsp
1 tbsp	fresh lemon juice	1 tbsp
	cayenne pepper	

Preheat the oven to 190°C (375°F or Mark 5). Soak the burghul in 30 cl (½ pint) boiling water for 15 minutes to swell and absorb the liquid.

Heat the oil in a saucepan. Add the onion and garlic and cook very gently for 3 minutes, stirring occasionally. Add the curry powder, coriander and cinnamon, and cook gently for 2 minutes.

Add the onion mixture, pork and salt to the burghul and mix. Form into 12, oval-shaped cakes about 1.5 cm (¾ inch) thick and 7.5 cm (3 inches) long. Place on a lightly greased baking sheet and bake for 35 mins, turning half way through cooking time.

Meanwhile, make the dressing. Mix the yogurt with the mint and lemon juice, and season with some cayenne pepper. Refrigerate until required.

Warm the pitta breads under a medium grill for about 1 minute on each side. Slit each bread open to form a pocket. Half fill each with some of the shredded lettuce. Spoon a little yogurt dressing into each and arrange two hot pork cakes on top. Fill the sides of the pittas with a little more lettuce, add some slices of cucumber and tomato to each. Top the filling with a spoonful of the remaining dressing. Serve at once, wrapped in napkins.

Pork Balls with Angel's Hair Pasta

Serves 4

Working
(and total)
time: about
40 minutes

Calories
280
Protein
20g
Cholesterol
65mg
Total fat
12g
Saturated fat
6g
Sodium
360mg

250 g	pork fillet, trimmed of fat	**8 oz**	**1**	carrot	**1**
1 tsp	fennel seeds	**1 tsp**	**10**	black peppercorns	**10**
2 tbsp	finely chopped parsley	**2 tbsp**	**30 cl**	dry white wine	**½ pint**
1 tsp	fresh lemon juice	**1 tsp**	**2**	fennel bulbs, feathery tops attached	**2**
¼ tsp	salt	**¼ tsp**	**150 g**	capelli ' angelo (angel's hair pasta)	**5 oz**
	freshly ground black pepper		**30 g**	unsalted butter	**1 oz**
1	bay leaf	**1**	**1 tbsp**	grated Parmesan cheese	**1 tbsp**
1	onion	**1**			

Combine the pork, fennel seeds, parsley and lemon juice, season lightly. Set mixture aside.

Put the bay leaf, onion, carrot, peppercorns and wine in a pan and cover with boiling water. Bring to the boil, then simmer.

While the stock is simmering, wash the fennel and slice it very thinly, cutting out any stringy centre or tips; chop the feathery tops finely and reserve for garnishing the dish. Form the pork mixture into balls about the size of large marbles.

When the vegetable liquid has simmered for at least 10 minutes, plunge the fennel into the pan and simmer until cooked but still crunchy. Strain the contents; remove the fennel and the liquid and

discard the other ingredients. Return liquid to the pan, simmer, add the pork balls.

Bring a large saucepan of lightly salted water to the boil. Throw in the pasta and cook it until it is soft but still has a firm bite – about 4 minutes.

When the pork balls are cooked – about 5 minutes – add the fennel to warm through. Strain the pork and fennel, reserving about 4 tablespoons of the cooking liquid. Strain the pasta. Melt the butter in a larger saucepan, and add the pork, fennel and pasta. Divide among four plates, pour a tablespoon of the reserved liquid over each, scatter the Parmesan and the reserved fennel fronds over the top. Serve immediately.

Saffron Pork with Quail and Prawns

Serves 4

Working (and total) time: about 1 hour

Calories
380

Protein
22g

Cholesterol
75mg

Total fat
9g

Saturated fat
3g

Sodium
100mg

250 g	pork fillet, trimmed of fat and cut into eight pieces	**8 oz**
2	quail	**2**
1 tbsp	virgin olive oil	**1 tbsp**
1	red onion, finely chopped	**1**
250 g	Italian round-grain rice	**8 oz**
¼ tsp	saffron powder	**¼ tsp**
2	pinches saffron threads	**2**
½ tsp	salt	**½ tsp**

	freshly ground black pepper	
1–1.25 litres	unsalted chicken stock	**1½–2 pints**
1	green chili pepper, seeded and finely sliced	**1**
1	red chili pepper, seeded and finely sliced	**1**
4	large cooked prawns	**4**

Divide each quail in two by cutting down the back and up along the breastbone. Remove any innards that remain, wash the quail pieces and pat them dry with paper towels. Rub the quail with a little of the olive oil, then set aside.

Heat the remaining oil in a heavy paella pan or frying pan, and sweat the onion in it for 1 minute. Add the rice and sauté for about 1 minute, then add the pork and sauté the whole mixture for a further 2 minutes, until the pork is sealed. Add the saffron powder and saffron threads, season with the salt and some pepper, and pour on enough chicken stock or water to

cover. Bring slowly to the boil, then simmer the mixture gently for 35 to 40 minutes, adding the remaining stock or water as necessary and stirring occasionally. After 30 minutes, test the rice for doneness. When it is still a little hard but nearly cooked, add the chili peppers and prawns to heat through.

While the rice mixture is cooking, grill the quail under a hot grill until they are well browned – about 10 minutes. Transfer the rice and pork mixture to a large dish or individual plates and serve immediately with the prawns and quail to one side.

Roast Pork Salad with Mustard Vinaigrette

Serves 4

Working (and total) time: about 10 minutes

Calories 245
Protein 26g
Cholesterol 60mg
Total fat 14g
Saturated fat 4g
Sodium 270mg

350 g	cold roast pork	12 oz
125 g	salad lettuce leaves, washed and dried	4 oz
2 tsp	sherry vinegar	2 tsp
2 tsp	fresh lemon juice	2 tsp
2 tsp	Dijon mustard	2 tsp

1 tbsp	virgin olive oil	1 tbsp
1 tbsp	arachide oil	1 tbsp
15 g	chopped chives	1½ oz
½ tsp	salt	½ tsp
	freshly ground black pepper	

Divide the lettuce leaves among four plates. Slice the pork as thinly as possible and lay it over the lettuce.

Whisk the sherry vinegar, lemon juice and mustard together in a bowl, then add the olive and arachide oils, and continue to whisk the mixture until it is thoroughly blended. Add the chopped chives and season with the salt and some freshly ground black pepper, then pour the mustard vinaigrette over the pork slices and lettuce.

Suggested accompaniment: crusty bread.

Phyllo Parcels

Serves 4

Working
time: about
45 minutes

Total time:
about
4 hours
(includes
marinating)

Calories
280

Protein
23g

Cholesterol
70mg

Total fat
15g

Saturated fat
4g

Sodium
100mg

500 g	neck end or other lean pork, trimmed of fat and cut into 2 cm (¾ inch) cubes	**1 lb**
12.5 cl	red wine	**4 fl oz**
2	garlic cloves, crushed	**2**
1 tsp	fresh thyme leaves, bruised	**1 tsp**
1 tsp	mixed peppercorns, coarsely crushed	**1 tsp**

15 g	dried ceps	**½ oz**
½ tsp	salt	**½ tsp**
4	large spinach leaves, stalks removed, or about eight smaller leaves	**4**
2	sheets phyllo pastry, each about 50 by 28 cm (20 by 11 inches)	**2**
2 tbsp	safflower oil	**2 tbsp**
4 tsp	redcurrant jelly	**4 tsp**

Put the pork, wine, garlic, thyme, peppercorns in a dish. Cover, marinate in a cool place for 3 hours. Soak ceps in warm water for 20 minutes.

Drain the meat and dry. Reserve the marinade. Drain ceps, rinse, then dry and chop them roughly.

Sauté the meat in a dry frying pan over medium-high heat, turning regularly, for 20 mins, until browned and cooked through. Add the mushrooms, marinade and salt. Reduce liquid, meat and mushrooms should be completely dry, then remove from heat.

Plunge the spinach into boiling water, drain immediately, refresh under cold water and lay out in a single layer on paper towels.

Preheat the oven to 190°C (375°F or Mark 5).

Cut each phyllo sheet lengthwise in half. Position one strip with a short side towards you and brush it lightly with oil. Place one large spinach leaf at the end of a strip then a quarter of the meat mixture in a pile on the spinach. Lift one corner of the strip and fold it over the filling to meet the opposite long side, then fold the package towards the far end of the strip. Continue folding until you reach the far end. Repeat with remaining phyllo, spinach and meat.

Brush parcels with oil. Bake on a non-stick baking sheet until golden – 20 mins. Serve hot, with redcurrant jelly.

Cannelloni Stuffed with Pork and Ricotta

Serves 4

Working
(and total)
time: about
1 hour

Calories
460

Protein
28g

Cholesterol
45mg

Total fat
20g

Saturated fat
6g

Sodium
145mg

250 g	pork fillet, trimmed of fat and minced	**8 oz**	
60 g	sun-dried tomatoes	**2 oz**	
90 g	low-fat ricotta	**3 oz**	
30 g	fresh basil, finely chopped	**1 oz**	
	freshly ground black pepper		
8	cannelloni tubes	**8**	
90 cl	unsalted vegetable or chicken	**1½ pints**	

	stock		
	Pesto Sauce		
90 g	fresh basil	**3 oz**	
30 g	pine-nuts	**1 oz**	
3 tbsp	virgin olive oil	**3 tbsp**	
1	garlic clove	**1**	
30 g	freshly grated Parmesan cheese	**1 oz**	

Cut one of the sun-dried tomatoes into strips and reserve for a garnish. Chop the remaining tomatoes finely and mix them well with the pork, ricotta, basil and a little black pepper. Using your fingers, fill the cannelloni with this stuffing mixture.

To make the pesto, put the basil, pine-nuts, oil and garlic in a food processor or blender, and blend for 2 minutes. Add the Parmesan and blend again briefly.

Bring the stock to a simmer in a pan large enough to take the cannelloni in one layer. Using a slotted spoon, carefully put the cannelloni into the stock, and poach for 15 minutes, or until the pasta is soft and the stuffing feels firm. Drain, reserving the stock, and keep warm.

For the sauce, blend 4 tablespoons of the stock with 2 tablespoons of the pesto, and heat if necessary. Keep any remaining pesto for another use. Arrange the cannelloni on a warmed serving dish, pour a thick ribbon of pesto sauce over them and garnish with the reserved tomato strips.

Editor's Note: The cannelloni tubes used in this recipe do not require precooking before they are filled.

Rocket Meatballs

Serves 4

Working
time: about
25 minutes

Total time:
about
40 minutes
(includes
marinating)

Calories
170

Protein
22g

Cholesterol
70mg

Total fat
8g

Saturated fat
3g

Sodium
490mg

500 g	shoulder or other lean pork for mincing, trimmed of fat	**1 lb**
30 g	rocket	**1 oz**
½ tsp	ground allspice	**½ tsp**
½ tsp	salt	**½ tsp**
	freshly ground black pepper	
4 tbsp	plain low-fat yogurt	**4 tbsp**
2 tsp	balsamic vinegar	**2 tsp**

	Yogurt Dip	
4 tbsp	plain low-fat yogurt	**4 tbsp**
2 tsp	balsamic vinegar	**2 tsp**
1 tsp	coriander seeds, toasted and crushed	**1 tsp**
¼ tsp	salt	**¼ tsp**

In a food processor, mince the pork with the rocket, allspice, salt and some pepper. Form into 16 small balls. Blend the yogurt and balsamic vinegar in a bowl and roll the balls in this mixture; leave them to marinate for 15 minutes, turning occasionally.

Preheat the grill to medium high. Place the meatballs and marinade in the grill pan and grill for about 10 minutes, turning and basting from time to time, until golden-brown and cooked through.

To make the dip, mix the cooking juices from the meatballs with the yogurt, balsamic vinegar, coriander and salt. Serve the meatballs hot with the yogurt dip in a bowl alongside.

Suggested accompaniment: green salad including rocket or watercress.

Editor's Note: The meat used in this recipe should be very fresh, as this will require no binding agent. If rocket is unavailable, use watercress as a substitute – up to 60 g (2 oz) per 400 g (14 oz) of trimmed meat.

Pork with Chinese Cabbage in Steamed Buns

Serves 6

Working time: about 50 minutes

Total time: about 2 hours and 20 minutes (includes proving)

Calories 340
Protein 19g
Cholesterol 30mg
Total fat 14g
Saturated fat 3g
Sodium 450mg

300 g	cooked roast pork loin, trimmed of fat and cut into small dice	**10 oz**
15 g	fresh yeast, or 7 g (¼ oz) dried yeast and ½ tsp sugar	**½ oz**
250 g	plain flour	**8 oz**
1 tsp	baking powder	**1 tsp**
15 g	hard white vegetable fat	**½ oz**
1 tbsp	sesame oil	**1 tbsp**
250 g	Chinese cabbage leaves, finely	**8 oz**
	shredded	
1 tsp	salt	**1 tsp**
1 tbsp	safflower oil	**1 tbsp**
1 tsp	finely grated fresh ginger root	**1 tsp**
2	garlic cloves, finely chopped	**2**
90 g	spring onions, finely chopped	**3 oz**
1 tbsp	rice wine or dry sherry	**1 tbsp**
1 tbsp	low-sodium soy sauce or shoyu	**1 tbsp**
2 tbsp	hoisin or barbecue sauce	**2 tbsp**

Dissolve the yeast in 15 cl (¼ pint) of warm water; if using dried, mix the sugar and yeast together with 15 cl (¼ pint) of warm water and leave for 10 minutes, until foamy. Sift the flour and baking powder together, rub in the fat. Mix the yeast liquid into the flour and fat and knead well. Cover the dough loosely with film and leave until doubled in volume – about 1 hour.

Strike the dough to deflate it, divide into 12 balls. Roll into circles about 10 cm (4 inches) in diameter. Brush with sesame oil, fold over into semicircles and place on oiled greaseproof paper. Cover loosely and leave to rise for 30 minutes.

Steam the semicircles in a single layer, partially covered, over boiling water for 20 minutes.

Meanwhile, sprinkle the cabbage with the salt and set aside for 20 minutes. Rinse well under cold water, then squeeze dry in your fist.

Heat the safflower oil and fry the ginger, garlic and spring onions for 1 to 2 mins, stirring. Add the wine, soy sauce, hoisin, and the remaining sesame oil, then reduce until syrupy. Stir in the cabbage and the pork.

Serve the buns from the steamer with the hot pork mixture. Each diner takes a bun, splits it and spoons in some filling. Eat with the fingers.

Italian Meat Loaf with Tomato Sauce

Serves 6		
Working time: about 25 minutes		
Total time: about 1 hour and 10 minutes		

Calories 250		
Protein 28g		
Cholesterol 80mg		
Total fat 11g		
Saturated fat 4g		
Sodium 130mg		

750 g	pork fillet, minced	**1½ lb**	**2**	garlic cloves, finely chopped	**2**
1	garlic clove, chopped finely	**1**	**1 kg**	tomatoes, skinned and chopped, or 800 g (28 oz) canned plum tomatoes	**2 lb**
30 g	fresh breadcrumbs	**1 oz**			
1 tbsp	tomato paste	**1 tbsp**	**1**	fresh bay leaf	**1**
2 tbsp	dry white wine	**2 tbsp**	**2 tsp**	finely chopped sun-dried tomatoes	**2 tsp**
30 g	sun-dried tomatoes, finely chopped	**1 oz**		freshly ground black pepper	
30 g	fresh basil, finely chopped	**1 oz**	**45 g**	dried ceps, soaked for 20 minutes in warm water, or 250 g (8 oz) fresh mushrooms, chopped and sautéed until soft 15 g (½ oz) butter	**1½ oz**
	freshly ground black pepper				
	Tomato Sauce				
1 tbsp	virgin olive oil	**1 tbsp**			
1	large onion, finely chopped	**1**	**30 g**	fresh basil, torn into small pieces	**1 oz**

Preheat the oven to 180°C (350°F or Mark 4). Combine the pork, garlic and breadcrumbs with the tomato paste, wine, sun-dried tomatoes, basil and some pepper. Mix them well together. Line a 500 g (1 lb) loaf tin with greaseproof paper and press the pork mixture into it. Bake in the oven for 1 hour.

While the meat loaf is cooking, prepare the sauce. Heat the olive oil in a heavy frying pan and gently fry the onion and garlic until they are translucent – about 5 minutes. Add the tomatoes,

bay leaf and the sun-dried tomatoes; season with some black pepper, and cook over medium heat for 15 to 20 minutes, or until the sauce is reduced and well combined. Drain the ceps, if using, and chop them into pieces of roughly equal size. When the sauce is cooked, remove the bay leaf from the pan and add the ceps or mushrooms and the basil. Reheat the sauce to warm through the ceps.

Serve the meat loaf cut into thick slices with the sauce spooned round it.

Useful weights and measures

Weight Equivalents

Avoirdupois		Metric
1 ounce	=	28.35 grams
1 pound	=	254.6 grams
2.3 pounds	=	1 kilogram

Liquid Measurements

$^1/_4$ pint	=	$1^1/_2$ decilitres
$^1/_2$ pint	=	$^1/_4$ litre
scant 1 pint	=	$^1/_2$ litre
$1^3/_4$ pints	=	1 litre
1 gallon	=	4.5 litres

Liquid Measures

1 pint	= 20 fl oz	= 32 tablespoons
$^1/_2$ pint	= 10 fl oz	= 16 tablespoons
$^1/_4$ pint	= 5 fl oz	= 8 tablespoons
$^1/_8$ pint	= $2^1/_2$ fl oz	= 4 tablespoons
$^1/_{16}$ pint	= $1^1/_4$ fl oz	= 2 tablespoons

Solid Measures

1 oz almonds, ground = $3^3/_4$ level tablespoons

1 oz breadcrumbs fresh = 7 level tablespoons

1 oz butter, lard = 2 level tablespoons

1 oz cheese, grated = $3^1/_2$ level tablespoons

1 oz cocoa = $2^3/_4$ level tablespoons

1 oz desiccated coconut = $4^1/_2$ tablespoons

1 oz cornflour = $2^1/_2$ tablespoons

1 oz custard powder = $2^1/_2$ tablespoons

1 oz curry powder and spices = 5 tablespoons

1 oz flour = 2 level tablespoons

1 oz rice, uncooked = $1^1/_2$ tablespoons

1 oz sugar, caster and granulated = 2 tablespoons

1 oz icing sugar = $2^1/_2$ tablespoons

1 oz yeast, granulated = 1 level tablespoon

American Measures

16 fl oz	=1 American pint
8 fl oz	=1 American standard cup
0.50 fl oz	=1 American tablespoon

(slightly smaller than British Standards Institute tablespoon)

0.16 fl oz	=1 American teaspoon

Australian Cup Measures
(Using the 8-liquid-ounce cup measure)

1 cup flour	4 oz
1 cup sugar (crystal or caster)	8 oz
1 cup icing sugar (free from lumps)	5 oz
1 cup shortening (butter, margarine)	8 oz
1 cup brown sugar (lightly packed)	4 oz
1 cup soft breadcrumbs	2 oz
1 cup dry breadcrumbs	3 oz
1 cup rice (uncooked)	6 oz
1 cup rice (cooked)	5 oz
1 cup mixed fruit	4 oz
1 cup grated cheese	4 oz
1 cup nuts (chopped)	4 oz
1 cup coconut	$2^1/_2$ oz

Australian Spoon Measures

	level tablespoon
1 oz flour	2
1 oz sugar	$1^1/_2$
1 oz icing sugar	2
1 oz shortening	1
1 oz honey	1
1 oz gelatine	2
1 oz cocoa	3
1 oz cornflour	$2^1/_2$
1 oz custard powder	$2^1/_2$

Australian Liquid Measures
(Using 8-liquid-ounce cup)

1 cup liquid	8 oz
$2^1/_2$ cups liquid	20 oz (1 pint)
2 tablespoons liquid	1 oz
1 gill liquid	5 oz ($^1/_4$ pint)